"When a small market baseball team, like the A's, lacked funds to buy high salaried superstars, we left traditional scouting methods and embraced sabermetrics to uncover undervalued players who can contribute to winning games. For any business lacking time to develop A-player leaders, *Competent is Not an Option* delivers a boldly innovative solution by adapting player development methods from sports. It's a game-changer."

—Billy Beane, General Manager, Oakland A's

"'Do it better than it's ever been done before' is a core principle of my WinForever philosophy, and Art Turock does a tremendous job of taking the concepts he learned at our coaching clinics and translating them to the business world. *Competent is Not an Option* is a fantastic resource to help develop your talents and maximize your abilities."

—Pete Carroll, Head Football Coach, Seattle Seahawks

"*Competent is Not an Option* shows how perfecting everyday execution and improving a team's skill sets can get accomplished while simultaneously improving an organization's top and bottom lines. This is not a collection of sports analogies. You will learn ingenious ways to adapt sports teams' talent development practices to systematize the art of performing at the highest level."

—Jim Donald, CEO, Extended Stay; Former CEO, Starbucks

"Art Turock has hit the bulls-eye with his candid insight into the world of business seen through the eyes of how individuals and teams become successful in sports. I grew up in sports and these lessons have served me well throughout my business career. They will take you to the top of your organization. Thanks Art, but don't give away all of our secrets."

—Howard White, VP, Jordan Brand, Nike, Inc.

"As a sales team that has utilized Art's talent development practices for several years, we can attest that what's in store for readers is many 'aha' moments to challenge themselves and their teams to be the very best they can be and become unrecognizable to their current level of proficiency!"

—**Mike Crone, Senior Vice President of Sales, Wells Enterprises/Blue Bunny**

"I'm a big fan of *Competent is Not an Option*. My concept of "over learning" pushed our players to be their very best all the time. Read this book and learn what it will take to bring out the best in your people."

—**Don Shula, Pro Football Hall of Fame Coach**

"I appreciate Art Turock's willingness to share the concepts and principles that caused him to transform from a good competitor to a world-class athlete right before my eyes. Greatness awaits the participating reader."

—**Michael Waller, USA Track & Field Masters Male Athlete of the Year, 2009, 2010**

"Throughout my life, I have been surrounded by the finest athletes in the world. They understand the principle that 'Practice Makes Permanent.' If you dare to prepare for outstanding performance, you will rise above mere competence to the level of a consummate professional. In *Competent is Not an Option*, Art Turock lays the foundation for individuals and organizations to attain truly world-class performance."

—**Peter Vidmar, Olympic Gold Medal Winner; Past Chairman of the Board of USA Gymnastics**

"In hunker-down times, many businesses are driving themselves to death by overemphasizing efficiency. *Competent is Not an Option* is a must-read for leaders who want to look at talent development from a new perspective where a team's capabilities improve each day as work gets done."

—**Thom Crosby, CEO, PAL'S Sudden Service; Malcolm Baldridge Winner**

"When our people walked into the meeting room, if a customer described their performance as 'competent,' they would interpret that to mean an A grade. Art, when you finished your program 90 minutes later, competent meant a C. Our people realized there was a higher standard we were capable of working toward— to be elite performers in customer responsiveness. *Competent is Not an Option* delivers the same impact for readers."

    —Roger Junkermier, CEO, Cerium Networks

"This book accurately portrays coaching as a crucial element in building superior organizational capabilities that constitute a game-changer strategy. Turock's coaching model intervenes at the root cause of resistance to behavior change—an individual's mindset—that limits possibilities for action and results. He provides practical guidelines for disturbing a coachee's blaming-infested mindset to instill a healthy disregard for what's mistakenly considered unreasonable effort and risk in behavior change."

    —Keith Cupp, President, Gazelles International

"I read *Competent is Not an Option* with non-stop wonderment. It is the first rigorous discussion I've seen that makes unique adaptations between sports' best practices for coaching physical movement with developing the mental and interpersonal skills used in business."

    —Len Rodman, Past CEO, Black & Veatch

"I always say the number one impediment to business transformation is mindset —and along comes Art Turock to show how to change it, individual by individual. Viewing people in business from the perspective of talent management, he shows how top-tier coaching in locker rooms can be brought to bear in companies from boardrooms to the frontline. If you are involved in personal or organizational transformation, avoiding this book is not an option."

    —B. Joseph Pine II, Co-author, *The Experience Economy
    *and Infinite Possibility***

"Art Turock is spot on with his book, *Competent Is Not an Option*. As a career Army Officer and Corporate Vice President, I have had over thirty years of experience observing elephants in the room that derail organizations from functioning at peak performance. I look forward to applying his innovative solutions to reach new elite performance standards in my growth as a leader and developing my team members."

—Barbara Trent, COL (R) USAR; *CEO, Altamira Technologies Corporation*

"If you want to run a successful company, you need to find and retain the best people for the job. As an effective leader, you must increase employee engagement by encouraging and helping people develop their talents to achieve higher standards and goals every day. This book shares a system that helps people reach their full potential."

—Douglas R. Conant, CEO, Conant Leadership; Former CEO, Campbell Soup Company

"In athletics, players and coaches constantly challenge themselves to get better, but in the business world we too often settle for being competent. *Competent is Not an Option* is the perfect book for business leaders who are in awe of how sports teams develop players' talents and want to know how to adapt their secrets to reach full performance capacity. Sports fan will love seeing their favorite athletes and teams as the subjects of case examples."

—Ken Lubin, Founder of Executive Athletes; Managing Director ZRG Partners

COMPETENT
IS NOT AN OPTION

Build an Elite Leadership Team
Following the Talent Development
Game Plan of Sports Champions

ART TUROCK
Elite Performance Game-Changer

Printed in the United States of America

Published by Pro Practice Publishing
Kirkland, WA

Library of Congress Cataloguing in Public Data
Turock, Art. Competent is Not an Option: Building an Elite Leadership Team by Following the Talent Development Game Plan of Sports Champions—
ISBN-13: 978-1497486935
ISBN-10: 1497486939

First edition

OTHER BOOKS BY ART TUROCK

Invent Business Opportunities No One Else Can Imagine

Getting Physical: How to Stick With Your Exercise Program

CONTENTS

FOREWORD BY DR. KEN BLANCHARD

I've been a big fan of Art Turock ever since he wrote *Getting Physical* in 1984 and helped develop an extensive health and wellness program for all our employees. The program's unique feature was Art's focus on mindset, particularly the distinction between *interest* and *commitment* in obtaining desired results. Interested people make excuses why they don't do what they say they're going to do. Committed people keep their commitment—no matter what.

Competent Is Not an Option is all about helping business leaders—whether they are CEOs, business owners, sales VPs, Human Resource Development and Learning VPs, or front office executives of sports teams—take their interest in developing an elite, high-performing organization and make it into a commitment they will keep.

As a leadership consultant, entrepreneur, and sports fan, I love this book. It's a fun read for business leaders like myself and my clients who wish they could develop the talent around them as effectively as the coaches of their favorite winning sports teams. Instead of citing only business case examples, Art shows corporate leaders how to adapt practice methods used by great athletes like Olympic swimming gold medalist Michael Phelps and future Basketball Hall of Famer Kobe Bryant. He also gives us the inside story about the player development process of winning coaches such as Pete Carroll of the Seattle Seahawks, 2014 Super Bowl Champions, and Nick Saban of the University of Alabama Crimson Tide, three-time BCS National Champions—things you don't hear about on ESPN.

Like no other leadership development book I have ever read, Art's translation of best principles and practices from sports make *Competent Is Not an Option* unique and relevant. The secrets sports teams know about—mindset shifts, practice methods, and elite talent development habits—aren't taught in any business school or corporate training department. I was particularly struck by Art's ability to teach deliberate practice methods you can use to build your organization's leadership capacity instantly while real work is getting done. Many of his techniques take only one minute. Instead of racing to do daily tasks more efficiently, you will be able to transform your work process into a permanent practice field for ongoing learning and development. Wow!

What qualifies Art to write such a cutting edge book? First, he is an outstanding performance coach. Whenever I have wanted to accomplish something where I knew I needed to keep my commitment, I would contact Art. His coaching has been key to my own fitness turnaround, which is well-documented in my recent book *Fit at Last: Look and Feel Better Once and for All*. Not only did I lose over 40 pounds, but I also improved my aerobic condition, strength, balance, and flexibility. I could not have done it without Art pushing me toward elite status for my age. As you'll read, *Competent is Not an Option* describes a number of condensed coaching conversations Art has had with individual executives and entire leadership teams. Second, Art is a great learner. He attended Pete Carroll's football coaching clinic four times to really absorb the Win Forever philosophy that inspires his players and coaching staff to aim to perform their player development processes better than any sports team in history. These learnings were central to Art developing his Learning-While-Working Process that helps business leaders ignite the latent leadership capacity in themselves and their top management teams.

Enjoy and apply what you learn from this book. It will make a big difference in your development as a leader, and in the lives of people with whom you interact— at work, at home, and in your community.

You've delivered on your promise to write a pass-along book, Art. Thanks.

Ken Blanchard

Co-author of *The One Minute Manager®* and *Leading at a Higher Level*

CHAPTER 01

INFLATED SENSE OF COMPETENCE: A LETHAL SABOTEUR

How do we develop an elite leadership team when there's barely enough time to get the day's work done? This question is the crux of what business leaders view as an insurmountable problem inherent with being in business. It is also the opening to a solution—solve *that* dilemma, and you change the game.

This game-changer opportunity requires looking in a different direction, viewing the workday and the development of leaders in a new way. The best place to look for solutions is in disparate fields, such as sports, where delivering elite performance is expected without question.

As an "elite performance game-changer," I challenge senior executives to build an organization saturated with leaders who not only produce extraordinary business results but also develop a team of elite performers. While leading seminars, coaching executives, and facilitating year-long leadership development projects, I see plenty of evidence that business leaders *don't believe* they can achieve this double win—developing a team of leaders who deliver near -term results while also developing good managers into great leaders. Why? They mistake their repeated success, documented in quarterly results, as evidence to dismiss any need to expand their team's leadership capabilities in order to achieve breakthrough results. They milk the winning formula that works wonderfully in today's market conditions, and settle for a group of competent leaders plus a few elite performers who've stopped getting better. No one realizes their enormous hidden reserves of leadership capacity not being expressed. Most leaders never master perhaps the most vital and under-valued facet of their role—developing extraordinary leaders and leadership teams.

However, before I could recognize this damaging tendency in my clients, I had to discover it in my own life far away from any corporate headquarters.

My First Wake-up Call:
Discovering the Compromise of Competence

My wake-up call, or what I think of as a *mindset disturbance*, began in 2006 when I took up sprinting as a new hobby at age fifty-six. "Why?" you are certainly asking, "would someone with no prior track background, suddenly start sprinting?" After all, by age fifty-six, flexibility is in decline, testosterone is in short supply, and fast-twitch muscle fibers are shot (for those of us who ever had fast-twitch muscle fibers).

Actually, I was motivated by the fundamental counter-intuitiveness of being a sprinter after midlife. Watching the local sports report on TV one night, I witnessed a 94-year-old man run 100 meters in 22 seconds. "Awesome," I said to myself, but it didn't end there for me. I became intrigued by an emerging challenge. After decades of gym workouts, I figured I was in terrific shape, but wondered what capacity I would have for sprinting. Most adult fitness programs emphasize cardiovascular fitness and running long distances, but sheer sprinting speed is missing. So I established my own time frame, the same four-year training period as an Olympic athlete, to discover my capacity for speed.

In the early phase of this challenge, I discovered that my gym workouts and perceived excellent conditioning didn't translate to the physical demands of sprinting. I couldn't run fifty yards and back to the starting line more than a few times without being winded—or as athletes say, "sucking wind." When I ran my first 200-meter dash in cleats, as I reached the home stretch my legs felt rubbery, and my finishing kick resembled the gait of a staggering drunk. At times, my workouts, designed by my coach, Les Black, felt more like Navy Seal survival training exercises.

More than four years later, and on the other side of my experiment, I am no longer a winded, rubbery-legged novice. In addition to astounding my physician with my physiological improvements, my time for the 200-meter dash qualified me for the 2009 and 2011 National Senior Games. In 2010, I ran the 60-meter dash indoors in All-American Standard time. In 2011, I took up the pentathlon, adding four more events—long jump, discus, javelin, and 1500-meter run—to my repertoire. In my first season, my pentathlon score ranked fourth in America in the men's 60-64 age group. I continue to compete and to inject periodic challenges in my training. I replicate workouts of professional athletes, such as running wind sprints up Walter Payton's Hill in Arlington Heights, Illinois, which is about fifty yards up a steep incline, and which I did twenty times.

I don't cite these achievements to impress you, but to establish the undeniable before-and-after results, which beg the obvious question: *Where did I find this hidden reserve of physical capacity?* Back then, before I gave a solid answer, I raised a more disturbing question: *Where else in my life am I assuming I'm giving my best effort—but I'm not even close?"* An unflattering truth emerged as I confronted this question. My answer was: my professional development as a speaker, writer, marketer, and executive coach, and also my relationships, including my marriage. I had accepted without questioning the trade-off of time to develop a successful career at the expense of cultivating close friendships. For years, I had taken my marriage for granted, investing little toward deepening our emotional connection. And truth be known, I was no longer improving my professional skill sets.

Because I was successful and basically satisfied with my accomplishments, I didn't take seriously these seemingly tolerable compromises. My months of soul-searching reached a crescendo when I read these words of Albert Schweitzer: "The tragedy of life is what dies inside a man while he lives."

I had repeatedly sold out on my full potential, and I tolerated competence, a compromise which kept me from making a concerted effort to raise my aspirations and to enjoy a greater sense of fulfillment. I compromised and settled for competent performance by making choices undermining my own motivation for getting better. I chose not to raise my performance standards, nor invest time and effort in activities vital to improving results, but which I didn't find compelling or fun. I opted to get better in several initiatives to advance my career, while my personal life was put on hold to wait its turn. I chose to steer clear of confronting my fears about behavior changes that might require unreasonable effort, or possibly even lead to failure. Once I realized I was choosing to protect my sense of competence, I understood I had confused being competent and sufficiently successful as evidence I couldn't possibly perform any better. I took accountability for my part in this story.

Mindset Disturbance #1

Since Albert Schweitzer wasn't a management consultant, he didn't realize that the tragedy of a business's life is the hidden reserves of employees, whose talent never gains expression, while the company endures.

Pause briefly before you make the first courageous step in taking accountability for *your part* in your story. Reflect honestly on these questions:

- What choices are you making that originate from your own acceptance of competence *as good enough*?
- How does this compromise of your full leadership capacity impact your team or even your entire business?
- Where might you have hidden reserves of performance capacity you're intrigued to discover at work and in your personal life?

Awareness is the first step to curing the *compromise of competence*, and in my case, a transformational makeover for my life ensued. I gained a destiny-shaping lesson. By creating a façade of near-optimal performance, I had undercut my potential. Now, every day is a journey into the sheer intrigue of redefining personal bests in my business and personal pursuits.

I share my story to illustrate the precarious situation we all face in cultivating and expressing our full capacity. This journey requires making a critical mindset shift. If I hadn't watched the ninety-four-year-old sprinter race, asked a disturbing question, and then internalized Schweitzer's quote, the rest of my life would've been a sad, "This is as good as it gets" flat line. Instead, I've drawn a line in the sand: *Competent is not an option.*

Waking up from my own sleepy waves of inflated competence, I noticed a lot of slumbering company among my clients. Since you chose to read this book, I suspect you're a lot like them—highly accomplished with a hunger to get better. I know just how incredibly close you are to tapping into hidden reserves of capacity that will enable you to surpass your previous best performance. I encourage you to treat the time you spend reading this book as preparing yourself to orchestrate a defining moment in your development as a leader. While anyone who aspires to be an elite performer will benefit from this book, I wrote it especially for CEOs, members of senior management teams, and their direct reports, who occupy high-impact roles where competent performance *is not an option.* My ideas are tailored for business leaders who want to expand their role to include developing good managers into great leaders, and great leaders into legendary ones. They also want to build a strong bench of elite leaders, so succession proceeds seamlessly.

Inflated Sense of Competence: A Lethal Saboteur

Assessing the upper limits of performance capacity is a tricky proposition. Business leaders' exaggerated sense of competence is a lethal saboteur of their organization's potential for great achievement.

Most of us think the term *competent* indicates we're doing a good job. However, "doing a good job" is only one interpretation for the meaning of competent. Think about it. What does competent mean to you? How does being competent make you feel?

Webster's Dictionary[1] defines competent as "well qualified; capable; fit; sufficient; adequate; able." These definitions bring others to mind: meeting expectations, average, status quo. Do these meanings inspire you and get your blood pumping faster? Or do they leave you feeling limited as a leader, and disappointed as an achiever?

It's vital you understand *why* our interpretations of competence matter. Most managers view competent performance as a safety zone. It's a place where, so far, we haven't stuck our necks out, causing us to suffer embarrassment from public failure—the undeniable signal of the need for course correction. Any private sense of failure to improve can be dismissed. After all, competent is good enough. However, mistakes in front of others call for us to acknowledge a problem along with the expectation of improvement. All too often, we hide out from undertaking action where our competence isn't certain.

Imagine you're a Senior VP of Sales who encounters this situation. Your sales team complains about an increase in administrative duties that cut into their time for selling. Your company attempts an obvious solution--hire more administrative staff to process electronic orders. Easy!

Nevertheless many sales reps continue to input their own electronic orders. These sales reps know what they need to do in actual sales calls to increase revenues from key customers—but don't do it. And the managers who are responsible for coaching these sales reps suffer from the same affliction. Although these managers are trained in coaching skills to improve their team members' performance, they often accompany the reps on calls and make the sale themselves.

Why?

This "imaginary" problem I posed for you to consider occurred at one of my clients, a global Fortune 500 company. I asked Laura, the vice president of sales about her team's chief pain point, she said, "We have duplication of roles. We have super salesmen who pitch in to do the work of sales reps to meet the quarterly numbers. We have sales reps who help out with administrative duties when we're short-handed."

I noticed "pitching in" was always in the direction of doing familiar tasks in order to avoid challenging ones. Pitching in didn't lead to sales managers who take time for coaching sales reps to overcome their reluctance to use newly-trained selling skills. Pitching in didn't lead Laura and her senior sales executives to address the lack of proper coaching of their direct reports, the front line sales managers.

The label "duplication of roles" covered up a more serious problem—a bunch of fearful people being permitted to underperform their job descriptions. The sales reps feared being found incompetent. So they engaged in undermining behaviors, which employ their well-honed strengths and fit in their comfort zone. Fear of showing incompetence causes an epidemic of undermining behavior, with sales reps and sales managers going AWOL from their jobs.

Here's an alternative and deliberately provocative interpretation to the phenomenon of someone becoming attached to being competent:

Achieving competence is the enemy of continuous improvement and great achievement.

Since we want to be seen as competent, we usually have a predictable process to get work done and to solve problems, and consequently we perform tasks the same way, every time. We follow the same familiar pattern, until it doesn't work any longer. It's what makes us reliably competent. We believe there's no compelling need to change, so trying something new to improve, which includes a risk of failure or making mistakes, goes outside our comfort zone where we adhere to our customary formulas for success.

Being competent is a professional liability when we have an emotional investment in appearing competent to ourselves, to our bosses, and to our team members. When our performance is less than competent, we interpret the situation as a threat to our professional identity and self-worth. It's safer to think we've reached our peak performance, rather than stretch to get better, since we're likely to appear incompetent at the outset of making any complex behavior change.

Do you see the irony in this misguided cost-benefit analysis? We're choosing to be limited by our own success. When we achieve competent or slightly better standards, we mistake this status as a signal to relax efforts to move the needle on our performance capacity.

However, this commitment to preserve our sense of competence at all costs comes with a serious downside. When we feel apprehension over appearing incompetent, we extinguish opportunities to learn, stretch, and grow.

The opposite is also true. When we embrace the experience of being incompetent, we ignite opportunities to develop new capabilities. We can accept temporary setbacks tied to attempting stretch goals because we are driven by a bigger purpose—continued learning and development as a leader.

Failing and learning from such failure is actually the precursor to succeeding beyond our wildest dreams. How's that for a mindset disturbance?

Disturbing the Compromise of Competence Mindset

I am continually amazed by the power of mindset disturbance, especially when it alters how we gauge the importance placed on being competent. I visited with Roland, senior vice president of operations for a world-renowned engineering and construction company, in his office after I presented a full-day seminar at his firm. I assumed Roland wanted to debrief about how he thought the seminar went. Instead, when he sat down at his desk, he broke into tears. Composing himself, he apologized and began to explain an unsettling discovery he made from the seminar regarding his leadership strengths and weaknesses. Roland had been with the firm for over forty years, most of it in the electric power division. He was now at the end of his career, close to retirement, and he'd recently been transferred to the telecom division. Roland was struggling with the formidable challenges contained in this role transition. He was known as a leader whose primary strength was being the go-to guy with expertise.

Roland confided, "When questions came up, I had the answers. I led by example, rolling up my sleeves and doing whatever it took to get the job done on time and on budget. Now, here I am in the last phase of my career, and the leadership style and skills I've relied on in the past, the ones that got me to this point, don't work in my new position. The ever-changing telecom business isn't like the predictable power-plant business. In the past, I used my experience to take any power-plant project and plan the necessary sequential activities, from preparing the original proposal to completion. While I know project management, I don't know the intricacies of fast-track telecom projects, which require keeping up with technical advances. In today's seminar, I realized if I keep trying to lead in the same way, I will hurt my company. I must depend on my team's expertise to guide decisions."

Roland was describing a mindset disturbance that revealed uncomfortable blind spots. Mindset disturbance is exactly what it says. It bothers you, makes you uneasy, forces you out of the comfort zone that you've maintained by settling for competent performance, and it moves you headlong into new challenges. It frees you to embark on new courses of action, just as it pushed Roland, and into making changes necessary to develop an inspiring sense of both humility and confidence—prerequisites for ongoing learning and growth.

As uncomfortable as it was for Roland to contemplate losing status and floundering on the job while learning to lead in new ways, he could see how being a leader who supplies answers was an antiquated winning formula. Roland was now free to operate with an open, learner's mindset—one which would enable his team members to contribute their expertise.

Seth Godin, a renowned marketing guru, wrote, "I think the incompetents among us are stars in the making."[2] He uses the words "serial incompetents" to describe individuals who want to keep getting better. I'll make the point even stronger:

> *The nobility of incompetence: Being incompetent*
> *is the make-or-break prerequisite for becoming*
> *an elite performer.*

My Second Wake-up Call: Seeing Leadership Development from a New Lens

For years, I could only translate my discovery of the compromise of competence to individuals who were pursuing elite performance. I couldn't articulate the organizational implications. Then I had my next wake-up call.

It happened in 2008 while I was participating in a series of fantasy football camps led by Head Coach Pete Carroll of the University of Southern California (USC) Trojans. I signed up for the sheer enjoyment of being part of a football training camp atmosphere, and to get an insider's view of a major college football program. I learned so much and had such a great time, I ended up attending four fantasy camps.

I vividly recall sitting in the team meeting room in Heritage Hall as the coaches described their player development process. USC's strength and conditioning coach, Chris Carlisle, walked to the lectern, wearing a t-shirt bearing the slogan, "Pain is certain. Suffering is optional." I had no idea his forty-minute talk would forever alter my mindset about cultivating talent. Carlisle spoke about the "prepare stage" of the overall player development process. Carlisle takes Coach Carroll's requirements for fundamental abilities—such as the target speed for wide receiver to run ten or twenty yards, or the specific hip flexibility movements to be ingrained in defensive backs' muscle memory—and customizes conditioning programs. Carlisle adamantly mandates preparation as a prerequisite for practice. "I teach athletic movement so our coaches can coach football. Since they don't have to teach complex and high-speed movements during practice, they can emphasize things like game strategy to counter an opponent's tendencies."[3] USC players are not allowed to practice without possessing football basics, and they're expected to refine these skills over their college career.

My mind flashed to the cavalier attitude toward leadership fundamentals I see in most businesses. Senior management and emerging leaders are presumed to have mastered basic leadership capabilities, which aren't a part of their technical knowledge in marketing, operations, sales, or medicine. These basics, including team decision-making, idea generation, presentation skills, listening, giving feedback, and running meetings, often aren't taught in business schools. A leader's preparation might involve reading books, attending a training course, or mentoring by a colleague who hopefully provides a great example. There are rarely formal mechanisms to assess daily improvement of these basics. There's no one to fill the role equivalent to football's strength and conditioning coach, who's both an expert and fully accountable for customizing ongoing improvement of leadership fundamentals.

I wondered, "Does this haphazard preparation qualify anyone for a seat in the boardroom?" As leaders assume larger responsibility, their deficient leadership basics create serious limits on their ability to wield proper influence.

The connections didn't stop there. From that moment on, I turned a fantasy football camp experience into a leadership development program in football cleats. I drew contrasts between USC's player development process and typical methods used for comparable development tasks in business. I asked myself, "How would it look if a football team copied the competent talent-development practices used in business?" The result was this chart:

Figure 1.1 — A Football Team's Adaptations of Comparable Business Practices

Comparable Processes	Practices Accepted as Competent in Business	Football Team's Adaptation of Business Practices
Warm-up for work	Employees go straight to daily tasks.	No pre-game warm-up is held.
Debriefing a just completed activity	When an account team completes an out-of-town sales call, they have a short conversation about "how do you think the call went?" before bolting for the airport.	Coaches don't review game films.
Executing a plan for a key event	Sales people deliver a standardized sales presentation, saturated with bullet-laden PowerPoint slides to cover in 60 minutes. They are essentially reviewing an outline and hoping the buyer doesn't offer unique objections or questions.	Coaches script dozens of plays in the offensive game plan and execute them in sequence. The quarterback and coaching staff don't improvise to counter an opponent's unanticipated formations.
Practicing for a key event	Preparation for key customer meetings gets done at the 11th hour, with little rehearsal to refine a team's coordination in delivering the presentation. Winging it is the norm.	Coaches pass out the game plan for study the night before the game, then walk through plays in a hotel conference room hours before kickoff.
Training Practicing	Seasoned employees detest role-playing, contending, "Role-plays are hokey compared to my real work experience." Managers give them a pass.	Upperclassmen are excused from practice, since they've run the plays many times in actual games.
Coaching	Managers are responsible for coaching to develop team members and for guiding implementation of operational plans. The trick is to somehow allocate time to do both tasks. Time for coaching is more a luxury, so it rarely gets done.	Coaches put higher priority on doing operational tasks (i.e., cleaning uniforms, mowing fields) than coaching the players.
Mastering the Basics	Senior managers are presumed to be competent to perform basic leadership skills, and don't need additional practice.	Coaches suspend their strength and conditioning programs.

Mimicking these common business practices produces a football team that is designed to get *the least performance* out of its players' talent. And yet business leaders reluctantly settle for a severely compromised leadership development process featuring:

- Debriefing without referring to formalized performance standards
- Using one-size-fits-all scripted presentations
- Winging it instead of preparing adequately
- Allotting insufficient time for coaching
- Excusing executives from practice designed to improve performance because of seniority
- Having no systematic warm-up routine to prepare to give a peak performance.

After creating the chart, I realized I'd been operating with a gigantic blind spot. During two decades of speaking and consulting in a range of industries, I hadn't noticed the grossly ineffective approach companies take to leadership development. I knew my clients could do a better job of developing leaders, but figured they were doing as well as could be expected under tough circumstances. I was wrong, and this was an "I was blind but now I see" revelation.

This new way of seeing leadership development came from filtering my observations of business as seen through a sports-performance lens. Coaches in football and other sports accept no compromises when it comes to player development. Along with the performing arts, sports are as close as it gets to being a pure performance field. Nearly 100 percent of a coach's time is devoted to player development. In the offseason, coaches seek to upgrade their methods of player development. In team sports, like football, basketball, and hockey, coaches expect their players to get better each week or each month of a season so their performance peaks when championships are on the line. *How many senior management teams do you know where members are expected to get better in leadership skills week after week?* Sports teams are an ideal field to study for anyone who aspires to build an all-star team of leaders.

The Leadership Development Game Plan

Most business leaders don't think of sports as a source for leadership development insight—but we should. What sports teams know about mindset shifts, world-class practice methods, and designing an elite talent development process isn't taught in any business school or corporate university.

What if you could cultivate the same competitive advantage to overcome your competition as sports leaders do to dominate their rivals? Imagine if you could operate like a legendary sports coach who views talent development from a sports-performance lens, which galvanizes these three interlocking roles and capabilities:

1. *Mindset master.* A leader whose power emanates from the mindset of a champion, and who also instills the same mindset in the team.

2. *Deliberate practitioner.* A leader who arranges practice regimens so team members have short-lived plateaus and will keep redefining their upside potential.

3. *Orchestrator of elite habits.* A leader who designs and executes a work process where everyone builds capabilities while real work still gets done.

With the insights I'd gained from my two wake-up calls and my client engagements, I conceived a pragmatic process, the *Leadership Development Game Plan*, an approach for cultivating these three roles that define an elite leader who galvanizes a team's leadership capabilities. In this process, there is no compromise of competence.

What's ahead?

Studying this book prepares you to implement three leadership roles in sequence from *mindset master* to *deliberate practitioner* to *orchestrator of elite habits*. Think of this progression as necessary to qualify for a series of prerequisites. The progression of prerequisites empowers you to exert influence on leadership development at an increasingly larger scale in your organization. You'll begin by working on yourself to develop an elite performance mindset, which empowers you to instill excellent practice routines in one-on-one coaching, and ultimately to redesign your organization's entire work process.

The *Leadership Developmental Game Plan*, which I adapted from sports, contains three parts that comprise this book's organizing framework. It's a game-changer strategy.

In **Phase 1: Generate the Mindset of an Elite Performer**, you will start by taking accountability for your mindset so it contains beliefs conducive to elite performance—instead of settling for being competent. Having the proper mindset is a make-or-break prerequisite for enabling your team to implement my counterintuitive leadership development practices with conviction, rather than dismissing them as impractical. In becoming a mindset master, you will develop an elite athlete's mental toughness, or ability to consistently perform near your upside performance capacity, regardless of prevailing circumstances.

In sports or in business, mindset mastery is vital to achieving the highest quality of performance. In baseball, a batter may possess the physical tools and knowledge of proper hitting mechanics. However, his ability to swing the bat to make solid contact suffers when he recalls his past struggles to hit a certain pitcher's split-fingered fastball. The hitter's mindset, which predicts a miserable plate appearance, interferes with executing to his full performance capacity. In business, many retail managers have the verbal skills and know the proper steps for delegation, yet they continue to micromanage out of fear their direct reports will make poor decisions that would tarnish their department's results. In both cases, mindset determines whether individuals use their knowledge and talent to execute to their full potential or fall short.

Mindset mastery involves making a habit of taking accountability for your mindset. You will learn a systematic approach to enlarge your own sense of what constitutes unreasonable effort and risk when you are redefining your sense of competence. You will get comfortable in enlarging your comfort zone. Best of all, taking accountability for your mindset will then spread to your team members, who will follow suit to discover new upside potential.

Phase 2: Practice Like a Pro shows you how to leverage behavioral science research on deliberate practice, an essential ingredient for gaining expertise. You'll learn how to conceive *deliberate practice* regimens, the most efficient way to hone capabilities, and eventually to function as an expert in your role, especially in building an all-star leadership team.

In becoming a deliberate practitioner, you will practice like a professional athlete. In my illustrations, you'll learn the deliberate practice methods of athletes like Kobe Bryant and Lindsay Vonn, and how they translate to your leadership development. You'll start with designing and fulfilling your own practice regimen so you continually improve your leadership skill proficiency. Ultimately, you'll extend your skills to help team members conceive unique practice methods to rapidly master long-standing plateaus. Eventually, you and your team will perform many facets of your roles with second-nature skill proficiency, without a trace of apprehension. Leadership development won't depend on managers setting the tempo because *every employee* will know how to practice to continually improve their performance.

Once you've become a deliberate practitioner, you're qualified to lead your entire organization in reinventing your work process so it's filled with opportunities for leadership development. In the last section of the book, **Phase 3: Orchestrate the Learning-While-Working Process**, you will learn how to orchestrate habitual routines into your daily activities so your managers are building leadership capabilities while real work gets done.

Iconic coaches in team sports (think of John Wooden, Nick Saban, Pat Riley, Tony LaRussa) use their player developmental process to cultivate habits that produce winning results, not for just one championship season, but for decades. Consequently, their teams continually improve over the course of a season— allowing the score on game day to take care of itself.

As an orchestrator of elite habits, you will design each day's work activities to be interspersed with triggering events that activate job-imbedded development routines. Mind-numbing meetings will be redesigned into engaging skill-practice sessions. Everyone will look for ways to refine leadership skills, even during phone calls, while giving PowerPoint presentations, and in the midst of breaks between meetings. The entire team will complete a task, and then promptly share their learning with direct reports, cross-functional colleagues, and even customers who might benefit. Ultimately, your organization will accomplish more hours of leadership development in a month than most teams do in a year.

Figure 1.2 – Overview of the Leadership Development Game Plan

Developmental Phases	Primary Tools	Leadership Role
Phase 1: Generating the mindset of an elite performer.	Taking accountability for your mindset	Mindset Master
Phase 2: Practice like a pro.	Four deliberate practice methods	Deliberate Practitioner
Phase 3: Orchestrate the Learning-While-Working Process.	Learning-While-Working Process	Orchestrator of Elite Habits

My ability to be your translator between two fields comes from being a practitioner on both fronts—business and sports. I've given speeches and conducted executive coaching sessions with leaders in 125 Fortune 500 companies, plus hundreds of trade associations. I've been privileged to orchestrate my signature Mission Unreasonable Project, a one-year program for senior management teams and sales managers who must reinvent themselves to address emerging challenges. Besides studying USC's player development process, I've received support in becoming a pentathlete from elite coaches, including one NCAA champion, two master's track world champions, and two former U.S. Olympians.

By embracing the roles of mindset master, deliberate practitioner, and orchestrator of elite habits, you gain access to your own hidden reserves of leadership capacity. You are making a courageous commitment to build your legacy as a leader. Since there is no guarantee you'll be competent in these new roles, your willingness to confront fear of failure marks you as elite leadership material. You will pioneer an innovative work process to produce unprecedented numbers of elite leaders. Your colleagues will be grateful to work in an environment designed to help them realize their full potential. Any day now, your leadership team will be ready to post this sign at office entrances to describe your organization's top prerequisite for employment.

In other words, competent is not an option.

PHASE I:

GENERATE THE MINDSET OF AN ELITE PERFORMER

Leadership Development Game Plan

Phase I:
Generate the Mindset
of an Elite Performer

Leader's role:
Mindset Master

Phase II:
Practice Like a Pro

Leader's role:
Deliberate
Practitioner

Phase III:
Orchestrate the
Learning-While-Working
Process

Leader's role:
Orchestrator of
Elite Habits

CHAPTER 02

ALL THERE IS AT WORK, IS TIME TO GET BETTER

Joe is CEO of a technology company that grew by leaps and bounds in its first decade. While it was exciting and energizing in the early years to be part of speedy growth and the challenges of conceiving innovative client solutions, Joe realized his team couldn't sustain the pace over time. Joe had intentionally hired talented, creative people, and was concerned they would leave the corporation as their excitement and adrenalin highs turned to frustration and depleted energy. He realized the company's strategy—"bring in all the business you can, and we'll figure out the rest when we have to," wasn't going to work much longer.

While the business had doubled, and daily workloads were being met, his management team was locked in a vicious cycle that didn't allow for their development as leaders. They had become competent at reacting to urgent priorities and meeting tough deadlines, often at the expense of never approaching the elite leadership performance standards they originally aspired to reach. The management team was gaining plenty of knowledge about their competition, products, technology, customers, and legal issues, but not the kind that would catapult their performance capacity as leaders. To maintain success for the long-term, Joe knew a different approach would be required, but he couldn't see a way for his team to break out of the cycle.

Joe's story is a familiar one. When my clients take the time to reflect on their company's future, they often realize developing their leadership team's capabilities is vital for continued growth and productivity. However, like Joe, most leaders think this ongoing need for development interferes with getting work done and consequently needs to take second place.

> *How do we develop leaders when there's barely*
> *enough time to complete the daily tasks?*

Maybe we need to reframe the problem, by asking different, counterintuitive questions:

- How does having a process for developing elite leaders become the best way we can keep growing as a company?
- How do we get near-term work done without sacrificing long-term goals and high-quality performance?
- How do we acquire new learning and improve our skill proficiency from every task we perform?
- How do we make leadership development a daily habit where all employees engage in self-coaching, in addition to receiving ongoing coaching from their boss?

An optimal solution to these issues for business leaders lies in the sports world, where coaches spend nearly all their time developing players to give outstanding performances during competitions. Elite coaches create highly regimented routines to help players break complex moments down to fundamentals, and view every practice drill as an opportunity for steady improvement to keep redefining their upside potential. Furthermore, teams need to get better week after week over the course of a season. Even during offseason workouts, players constantly need to shore up their weaknesses to develop a more robust skill set. In contrast to most businesses, sports teams have no time when they can coast and not attempt to get better.

What if we revised our beliefs about the nature of our work process, and embraced its potential as an ongoing field of practice for developing elite leaders? What if we adapted a best principle common to sports teams? *All there is at work, is time to get better.*

Reframing how you interpret your organization's work process is the beginning step to reinventing yourself as a mindset master capable of transforming a team of competent leaders into elite performers. In this chapter, we'll explore how your mindset defines your team's capacity for learning and the development of elite leaders. We'll learn from two case studies depicting the lengths that organizations must go to achieve continual leadership development that's the catalyst for industry-leading performance. These case studies come from unusual organizations—a baseball team and a fast-food restaurant chain.

Mindset Shift: Gaining Access to Your Full Leadership Potential

Asking a provocative question is like reaching for a key to unlock the door to a hidden, out-of-reach space. Sometimes opening the doorway, crossing the threshold, and entering that space can be disturbing and uncomfortable, but it can also be freeing.

I conceive my role as an instigator, and consider it my responsibility to persistently ask questions to encourage you to think in new ways about subjects you might prefer to avoid. I want to awaken you to blind spots and hidden abilities to gain access to your full leadership potential. When I ask, "How do you react to the word 'competent'?" or, "How would you describe a typical workday?" my goal is to lead you to discover new insights which are initially uncomfortable to recognize, but eventually free you to take extraordinary actions. When I inquire, "What if you thought of your leadership role as being the coach of potentially elite performers?" my purpose is to direct your attention to your mindset, something most people rarely pause to consider, even though mindset plays a make-or-break role in setting the upper limits of performance.

Your mindset is the source of your freedom

A mindset is a habitual, pre-ordained filter for interpreting and responding to our experience. The way you interpret a situation is shaped by two primary perceptual filters: one filter is *your view of the past*, which accounts for why things are the way they are, including history, recurring troublesome situations, and regrets. The second one is *your view of the future* or where things are going, including: predictions, expectations, and hopes.[1]

There are three interlocking aspects of mindset.

- Mindset is *automatic*. We don't realize the pre-programmed habitual nature of our interpretive bias in how we size up every situation.

- Mindset is *hidden*. We don't distinguish the interpretations, assumptions, beliefs that make up our mindset from actual facts. So our mindset, a totally subjective interpretive bias, is mistakenly regarded as reality.

- Mindset is *unexamined*. We are not aware of our mindset, so its content isn't subject to any assessment for accuracy or effectiveness.

Implicit in the words used to define mindset, such as "automatic," "hidden," and "unexamined," is a lack of awareness and, therefore, the explicit need to be more mindful, more aware. Unless we practice tuning in to the content of our mindset, it becomes the only interpretive bias for sizing up and responding to emerging circumstances for which we take no responsibility.

Our mindset determines how we experience a situation—either as a threat to constrain us, or as an opportunity to free us to take action. The way our mindset filters a situation determines how we feel, what we see, what we hear, what we choose, how we act, and ultimately our results.

Figure 2.1 — The Chain of Influence of Mindset

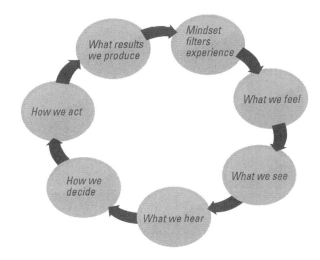

Notice the all-encompassing influence of mindset on our sensory experience, as well as our ensuing decisions, actions, and results. To the degree we're blind to the impact of our mindset, we lose our freedom of choice and our power to act, which then hinders our results. Here's the larger dilemma. We are blind to the fact that we are unaware of the content of our mindset. Without realizing it, we make choices that not only inhibit long-term results, but keep us from realizing the full expression of our natural talents.

The destiny-shaping impact of a mindset master

During a day-long seminar for telecom managers, I ask everyone to describe their daily work experience. This isn't a trick question. It's one I routinely ask when I make the shift from seminar presenter who imparts information, to one who models the role of a mindset master. I invite this group to share how they experience a typical work day, while I write their descriptions on a flip chart. The following list contains a sampling of what the managers say:

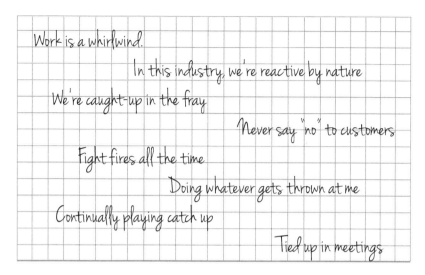

Leaders from a range of industries regularly use similar phrases, so I'm not surprised by what I hear. There is always a common theme—a lack of control, powerlessness in the face of daunting circumstances, and doing battle with nearly overwhelming difficulties in order to execute planned activities. I call it the siren song of victims of time deprivation.

After pausing to give everyone a chance to ponder the list, I tell them: "I don't work in your business, so I can see things from a different perspective. You think your interpretations represent the inherent nature of your work and the industry itself. But I hear them as a reflection of your mindset. In this group, there's so much agreement regarding how you experience work, it seems like the only way to interpret your circumstances."

One brave soul responds, "No, that is the reality of our business."

I continue to explain. "I'm not talking about the pace and constant demand to get more work done. I'm pointing out how your shared mindset—your interpretation —identifies this group as victims of a fast-paced, reactive work environment that's not about to slow down any time soon. You are blaming your day job for being an insurmountable obstacle to your leadership development and to improving your performance. By adopting this mindset, your workday becomes a steady stream of habitual routines you've come to view as necessary, sometimes heroic behaviors, to support efficiency and get near-term results. Unfortunately, these same behaviors undermine the development of high-performing leaders in the long term."

If we ask the efficiency-driven telecom managers where leadership development fits in their priorities, and then boil their responses down to one sentence, it might be:

Leadership development is an unfortunate
casualty of our daily business practices.

Operating from that mindset, these telecom managers must either engage in the normal operational duties of a workday or participate in activities geared to development. In this either-or trade-off, the habitual choice is get tasks done in the most efficient ways possible, such as:

- Micromanaging
- Pursuing easy tasks to avoid challenging ones
- Winging it style of preparation
- Multitasking
- Tolerating sticky problems
- Making fuzzy, inauthentic "I'll get back to you" agreements
- Failing to prioritize, or doing only urgent priorities
- Sticking to customary ways of performing tasks
- Never setting accurate expectations with customers

These behaviors become a preordained modus operandi, especially when a group's mindset is geared to merely survive a seemingly constant onslaught of activity.

My telecom managers group is far from unique in their mindset and correlated activities. In fact, most management teams regularly function without realizing they are operating in the default mode in order to get near-term work done as efficiently as possible. However, every minute spent consumed by stopgap, efficiency-driven habits undermines the ability to take concerted actions to accomplish vital long-term priorities, like leadership development. "Good enough, given all that's on my plate" becomes everyone's marching order. People fall in step with the mindless race to be efficient and competent. They grow resigned to tolerating a compromise—at least near-term results get done, even if they're putting the future in jeopardy.

The only way to derail the intensifying log jam of activities is to disturb a management team's victim mindset, and their accompanying visceral sense of being overwhelmed by a relentless, never-enough-time reality. Altering the way they interpret their situation actually unleashes the power to orchestrate an entirely different work experience and a new set of correlated actions, such as:

- Delegating tasks and decisions to develop a more highly skilled team that can take on greater responsibilities.

- Creating routines so that vital, but not urgent, activities get done consistently.

- Solving recurring problems so they no longer consume time.

- Determining the high-impact goals that make other activities easier or totally unnecessary.

- Negotiating and managing accurate customer expectations to eliminate time needed for recovery responses.

- Establishing standards for being prepared for sales meetings so customers notice the superior performance, and future sales become more likely.

Once leaders arrive at this discovery, and can make a mindset shift to reinterpret their experience in an empowering context, they feel exhilarated by a renewed sense of freedom. They can even take on the leadership role I was modeling—being a mindset master.

What separates mindset masters from the pack of leaders who develop merely competent direct reports and management teams? *Mindset masters treat a mindset as a fragile, malleable mental fabrication.* Distinguishing mindset as a mental fabrication, rather than mistaking it for reality, is essential to creating a new capacity for leadership. If Steve Jobs viewed his dismissal at Apple early in his career as evidence he lacked ability to run a mature company, he would never have staged his comeback to commandeer the innovation juggernaut. If CEO Howard Schultz believed coffee was a commodity product that could never sell for more than pennies per cup, he would never have founded Starbucks. If Coach Pete

Carroll viewed his firing by two NFL teams as proof of his failure as a head coach, he would never have reinvented himself as a leader who orchestrates elite habits in championship teams with the USC Trojans and the Seattle Seahawks.

If leaders can't see that their extremely busy workplace could be redesigned as a process filled with opportunities for learning and skill-building, they stunt their own growth as leaders, and also that of their organization. Mindset determines the destiny of leaders and the groups they lead.

Because mindset is only a mental fabrication, any self-limiting assumption can be replaced by a more empowering one. And it doesn't always take months of coaching sessions. Sometimes a single fifteen-minute coaching conversation like the one I had with the telecom managers is all it takes to generate a mindset shift.

> *The prevalent mindset, whether intentional or unintentional, influences an organization's upper limits in leadership development, producing plenty of either competent or elite leaders.*

The Leadership Development Mindset Shift

Leadership development is an unfortunate trade-off

"Talent is the No. 1 priority for a CEO. You think it's about vision and strategy, but you have to get the right people first."[2]

—**Andrea Jung, past CEO, Avon Products**

When I urge CEOs to set a goal that aspires to ensure 100 percent of their leaders become A-players or elite performers, I'm told in no uncertain terms, "100 percent is unrealistic." Then they revert to the usual deadly duo of culprits: time and money. "We can't afford to hire A-players, and we don't have the time to develop B-players into A-Players."

Can leaders really afford not to embrace the concept of developing 100 percent elite leaders? When *Good to Great* author, Jim Collins, conceived the famous phrase, "Get the right people on the bus, in the right seats," do you really think he was endorsing B-players and C-players as bus riders? No chance. He cites CEOs like Fanny Mae's David Maxwell, who threw down the gauntlet when he asserted the seats on the bus would be reserved only for A-level people willing to give A-plus effort. Collins explains:

> … if people board the bus principally because of all the other great people on the bus, you'll be much faster and smarter in responding to changing conditions. Second, if you have the right people on your bus, you don't need to worry about motivating them. The right people are self-motivated: Nothing beats being part of a team that is expected to produce great results. And third, if you have the wrong people on the bus, nothing else matters. You may be headed in the right direction, but you still won't achieve greatness. Great vision with mediocre people still produces mediocre results.[3]

How did leadership development come to be so misunderstood? The lack of A-players isn't due to lack of time or money. It's due to a seriously flawed leadership development process that's designed to produce merely competent leaders.

Most senior executives relegate leadership development as an unfortunate tradeoff. Their mindset allows only one alternative: develop people *or* get real work done. In the case of leadership development, efficiency in getting work done faces off against the long-term effectiveness of developing more proficient capabilities.

In balancing this trade-off of priorities, leadership development gets treated as a *work-around*, a temporary fix. A manager's primary role is to oversee an efficient work process. In turn, he or she arrange quick-fix training seminars, and shoehorn in random acts of development, such as occasional performance monitoring, coaching, and mentoring. Calendar-driven rituals like performance appraisals and 360-degree peer reviews get done. People reach inevitable performance plateaus, which are misdiagnosed as reaching the limits of performance capacity.

The leadership development trade-off is based on the erroneous presumption that everything possible is being done to develop leaders, given the frenetic pace to accomplish real work. *In actuality, we choose to do everything feasible to efficiently develop competent leaders. In the short-term, we're getting what we want. In the long-term, our efficiency destroys any chance we have of developing elite leaders.* By failing to take accountability for our flawed, efficiency-driven mindsets, we perpetuate these limitations.

The destructive impact of a mindset sanctioning the leadership development trade-off is well documented in research. In their book, *Making Talent Your Business*, Wendy Axelrod and Jeannie Coyle summarize research studies which spell out serious flaws in leadership development.[4]

- First, not much development is going on. One highly reputable firm specializing in leadership development studied how frequently each of 67 behaviors proven to make up good leadership got used on the job. "Developing others" consistently came out near the bottom of the list, located among the least-used leadership behaviors.[5]

- Second, managers are held accountable for business results, but not for developing their team members. Of the organizations studied, few held managers (only 7 percent) and executives (only 10 percent) accountable for *developing* direct reports.[6]

- Finally, only one manager in ten uses work itself as a developmental tool. This 1:10 ratio means 90 percent of managers fail to capitalize on the greatest source of leadership development—informal job experiences. Additional research at the Center for Creative Leadership (CCL) shows that 70 percent of leadership development comes from informal experiences, 20 percent from developmental relationships (a boss, mentor, trade association involvement, job shadowing a highly skilled manager), and only 10 percent from classroom or online training.[7] The 70 percent contribution of informal learning experiences stands out, and includes examples like covering for a colleague on leave, stretch assignments, coordinated role swaps, increased decision-making responsibility, and orchestrating a change initiative.

The message from this research is clear. Leadership development doesn't happen in a series of isolated leadership training classes, but requires plentiful on-the-job experience that affords numerous practice opportunities. If you consider how you master almost any skill—putting a golf ball, designing an inspiring presentation, mastering a new language—it takes lots of fully engaged practice, regular self-assessment, and feedback. To produce elite performers, leadership development must be an ongoing, on-the-job, daily process.

Given the enormous gap between current practice and elite conditions for leadership development, this trade-off isn't really about accepting a less-than-ideal solution as much as using face-saving language to conceal the lack of effective best practices. Business leaders can talk a good game about leadership development, but they can't deny their failure to develop top-flight leaders. Meanwhile, *development takes a shellacking at the hands of efficiency.*

Let's face the harsh truth right here, right now. You're not dealing with a time-management problem. Employing time-management techniques to cram more activity into a time slot is not a viable solution for producing elite leaders. Attempting time-management solutions got you where you are today—with leadership development lagging far behind daily work production. To escape this trade-off, you'll need to adopt a new perspective—one that changes how you understand and value leadership development, as displayed in the following figure:

Figure 2.2 — The Leadership Development Mindset Shift

From Customary Mindset of Competent Performance	To Transformational Mindset of Elite Performance
Leadership development amounts to sporadic activities—an unfortunate but necessary trade-off since producing near-term business results must assume top priority.	Leadership development happens every day, and is built into the work process. All there is at work, is time to get better—as a leader.

All there is at work, is time to get better as a leader

If your goal is to produce elite leaders, you will need to adopt a mindset shift that paves the way for designing a work process conducive to developing leadership capabilities every day. Accordingly, leadership development and real work become intertwined, rather than competing for attention. Developmental opportunities are available in any task, and are totally dependent on how mindful leaders orchestrate everyday activities into occasions for learning and development. This transformational perspective, captured in the have-it-all spirit of elite performance, can be condensed to one sentence: *All there is at work, is time to get better.*

With the mindset shift, "All there is at work, is time to get better," you will experience the impact of being able to identify new opportunities to continually refine leadership skills while getting real work done. It's important to note that these learning opportunities were there all the time, but you couldn't see them while operating from a mindset geared to look only for efficiency.

To help you notice new aspects of your work experience so you can capitalize on rich learning opportunities, I'm going to describe three best principles most businesses rarely apply:

Figure 2.3 — Best Principles to Capitalize on to Create Learning Opportunities

Best Principles To Be Mindful Of	Benefits Derived
Distinguish between "doing" and "learning" goals	To get the most benefit out of ever-present opportunities at work to get better, you will need to learn to value learning and performance improvement as an essential goal to pursue every day.
Draw contrast between free-form versus well defined, leadership skills	To notice leadership skills that are ripe for improvement, you will need to mindfully define the most effective way to perform various skills and accomplish tasks.
Conceive job-imbedded development routines available in daily tasks	To exploit the everyday occasions to practice for skill improvement, you will need to design a work process to build leadership capabilities while real work gets done.

The combination of these best principles creates superb conditions for elite talent development to occur. When everyone sets learning goals, knows the most skillful approach to take in every task, and adheres to routines that enable skill building to occur within the actual work itself, there is no need to settle for a leadership development trade-off.

Principle 1: Distinguishing Doing and Learning Goals
When you ask colleagues, "Besides getting our daily tasks done, what other valuable results come from work?" expect to receive blank stares. How many of your co-workers would claim work is jam-packed with occasions for non-stop learning and development?

When most people refer to *work*, they mean *doing* something—accomplishing a goal, performing a task, and checking off items on a to-do list. This "getting things done" aspect of work, I will call "doing goals." When managers set quantifiable goals, their first and only inclination involves measuring productive work that gets done. Telemarketers count sales appointments scheduled. Lawyers tally billable hours. A cashier's performance is judged by the average time spent per transaction. Advertising copywriters count clicks on ads placed on the Internet.

Beyond the obvious "doing goals," a second, largely unrecognized and underappreciated result of work is learning. "Learning goals" refer to gaining knowledge, building skills, gleaning fresh insights, and making mindset shifts.

To produce elite performers requires a special work process where "learning and doing goals" complement each other. "Doing goals" are paramount in the short-term. "Learning goals" bring about capabilities even more vital to addressing future challenges.

By adopting a mindset where learning gets legitimized as a valid outcome, work itself becomes a free-admission seminar. When everyone's alert to learning opportunities, teachers are plentiful. Customers teach us how to sell, how to deliver service, and how to solve problems. Direct reports help us learn to customize our coaching efforts. Competitors challenge us to get better, especially in strategic thinking. Bosses serve as good and bad models for leadership. Gatekeeper receptionists help sales professionals learn to build rapport in order to gain access to decision-makers. Sales professionals educate buyers with fresh insights about consumer trends, leading-edge technology, and wasteful operating practices. Co-workers who are difficult to work with provide abundant opportunities to practice stress management.

Once you become tuned in to the notion of learning goals, you'll find nearly every situation represents a potential teachable moment or learning opportunity. In the same way, people are already conscious of "doing goals," you will become just as aware of making progress on accomplishing a daily slate of "learning goals."

Principle 2: Drawing contrast between free-form versus well-defined basic leadership skills

The term "free-form basics" refers to occasions when managers perform their fundamental leadership tasks in their own idiosyncratic way, without adhering to a step-by-step process to guide their thinking and actions. When performance standards are spelled out, but are loosely monitored, managers make up their own abridged version of a process that is suited to their comfort zone. For example, managers who are uncomfortable giving corrective feedback only praise effective performance. Team members never learn what parts of their performance can be improved and how to go about refining their skill proficiency.

When an organization doesn't institute rigorous standards for leadership basics, managers are left to figure out their own methods and/or follow their colleagues, who might be using an effective or questionable approach. For instance, in conducting training intended to change behavior, managers often spend 90 percent of the time delivering PowerPoint presentations. Little time gets allocated for modeling the new skills to help trainees who learn best from visual demonstrations. Trainees rarely role-play to get the necessary feedback required to get a "hands-on" sense of the new skills. Managers repeatedly violate the fundamental training design to tell, demonstrate, and practice—all of which is essential when the learning goal requires going beyond imparting knowledge to actually changing behavior.

As a final example, Carol Burch and Chris Longridge of Girandole Enterprises[8] developed a decision-making software tool, Dwaffler, after observing that frequent miscues in free-form versions of decision-making often resulted in failure to:

- Articulate long-term and short-term decision criteria, especially criteria people are uncomfortable verbalizing.
- Describe the full gamut of long-term opportunity costs, which are largely invisible at the time of the decision.
- Rank the relative value of multiple-decision criteria.
- Explore a full range of viable solutions.
- Assess how proposed solutions stack up against weighted-decision criteria.

Does this list of flaws suggest to you any ways your team's decision-making process may need to be formalized? Many decisions turn out to be based on gut hunches, momentary emotions, untested assumptions, short-term considerations, and limited options. In the worst case, free-form decision-making amounts to rubber-stamping a CEO's decision, or caving in to the solution espoused by the team's most persuasive member.

Here's a simple test to see if your team employs free-form basics or a well-defined process. Before you embark on a task, ask team members to describe the sequence of steps to perform it effectively. If you receive almost as many different process descriptions as you have team members, your modus operandi for this task is a free-form basic.

Free-form basics run rampant in most organizations. Unfortunately, this lax standard of performance does not improve skills proficiency, nor does it produce optimal business results.

Principle 3: Conceiving Job-Imbedded Development Routines

The third best principle, conceiving job-imbedded development routines, sharpens awareness of the continuous opportunities to practice skills in accomplishing daily tasks. The trick is to make these opportunities into effortless routines. A routine is a regularly followed sequence of actions that becomes a habit. Job-imbedded development routines incorporate regularly scheduled, and spontaneously triggered, occasions for learning which interrupt the existing momentum to get work done.

Instead of tolerating a colleague's ineffective habits, a team arranges to have a ritual where any member can instantly signal to *Re-Do* a just-completed communication, and practice a more skillful response. For instance, when an entire group blames unfavorable circumstances for poor results, the meeting facilitator calls for a "Re-Do," and participants practice taking accountability for their actions that undermined the desired outcome.

Instead of enduring boring meetings, the new imbedded routine for meetings has at least one agenda item requiring the group to practice specific leadership skills. Imagine an entire senior management team designing their weekly meetings so each of their departmental teams practice skills like idea generation, problem -solving, or decision-making.

Job-imbedded development routines do not consume much additional time when they're interjected into real work. They often take minutes, sometimes seconds, to execute. Most often, a leader takes a few moments to structure the process so the learning and skill practice become a byproduct of the task being performed.

Job-imbedded development routines are different from developmental assignments. An "assignment" suggests an actual new job, promotion, transfer, or major revision of an existing job, like leading a newly formed cross-functional team. Thinking of development as requiring formal assignments limits the possibilities for advancing learning. In contrast, job-imbedded development routines don't require managers to take on new roles, locations, or responsibilities. Instead, practicing to build leadership skills is a permanent developmental assignment.

Implications for the three best principles.
These three best principles accompanying the mindset shift—all there is at work, is time to get better—enable you and your team members to participate in an extremely rare work experience. A productive day is measured not only by the quantity of tasks done, but by the amount of learning that takes place. Free-form basics get replaced with sanctioned performance protocols to cover leadership basics. Every task is viewed as a potential job-imbedded development routine where team members capitalize on potential learning from the experience.

Are you beginning to see a superior, perhaps a game-changer solution, to the leadership development trade-off? With this mindset shift, a breakthrough in performance becomes possible. Instead of an either-or trade-off, a double dose of productivity now becomes available. If 70 percent of leadership development results from on-the-job experiences, as shown in the CCL research cited earlier, then the best way to drive productivity is by orchestrating a double win—building leadership capabilities while real work gets done. Unprecedented productivity occurs simultaneously on two fronts: building skills while accomplishing daily tasks.

I first heard about this "double win" from sports psychologist Tim Gallwey, author of *The Inner Game of Work*, who wrote: "Work is a process of growing your capabilities, while in the process of producing results in order to be better able to produce future results."[9] No matter what work a team is doing, they discover how to maximize learning. Leaders create a process that beckons everyone to identify skill-building opportunities imbedded in the work itself.

Mindset Disturbance #2

Be ruthlessly honest. Reflect on these questions in order to master this leadership development mindset shift:

1. How effective are you at performing the part of your job that calls for developing leaders?
2. When you look at your direct reports' performances, are they getting better in their skills and knowledge each year, or remaining at the same level of proficiency and results?
3. What opportunities are lost when your team gets so absorbed in pursuing near-term results that they allow leadership development to slide?
4. Where do you hold back in growing your business because you don't have sufficient qualified leaders on the bench?

5. What problems are almost certain to develop in the future as your managers must lead larger teams and business units?

6. Where do you fear you might fail when you attempt to develop leaders?

7. What signs of past success can you use as evidence of your capabilities to develop leaders?

8. What part of your legacy as a leader is at stake when you consider the impact you can have on your colleagues' careers?

Case Examples of the Best Principles

The St. Louis Cardinals: Making superior talent development a competitive advantage

Since 1960, the St. Louis Cardinals have had consecutive losing seasons only once, 1994–1995. Their eleven championships occurred over five decades. No other baseball team can claim such a consistent stretch of winning seasons. The Cardinals' sustained success originates with defining and teaching basic skills for hitters, pitchers, and fielders. Every fundamental—hitting philosophy, bunt plays, pick-off moves—is taught the same way across the organization. There's no room for guesswork in exercising the right values in off-the-field situations. The baseball education offered in the minor leagues is designed to ensure players hear a message consistent with the one they will receive when they graduate to the Busch Stadium clubhouse.

Why is the Cardinals' talent development approach worth being deemed a game-changer strategy? To meet payroll allocations, major league teams compress the time that less-expensive, young players spend developing their skills in the minor leagues. In this way, any team executing a superior player development process gains a distinct competitive advantage.

Since purchasing the team in 1995, Bill DeWitt, Jr. has reinforced the Cardinals' long-standing priority placed on player development over buying free-agent talent. His front office staff executes this competitive strategy. Director of Baseball Operations John Vuch, says, "We're not going to always be able to out-talent teams. We have to make sure we're playing fundamentally sound baseball. We have to maximize the talent in that way by playing the game the right way. This organization always has." [10]

"We've realized long ago that free agency was not a place we wanted to be using our resources," says St. Louis General Manager John Mozliak. "We decided that for us to have sustained success, we had to do it internally."[11] A long line of Cardinal coaches formalized their player development methods in an 86-page "operations manual" called The Cardinal Way.

Have you ever been so curious about the nuances of the twelve different ground balls a second baseman might have to field that you wanted to study the subject? Or did you ever wonder about the position a catcher should take prior to receiving a 3-2 pitch? This isn't a case of baseball people who've gone anal in compiling minutia. These examples show the commitment to teach the level of detail necessary for superb player development.

Depending on talent development as a competitive edge, the team has produced phenomenal results. In 2013, five players drafted after the tenth round, and as far back as the fortieth round, contributed to the Cardinals winning the National League Championship. Being a late draft choice means every other team's scouting department found each of these five players lacking in natural talent, compared to the players drafted in the early rounds. Consequently, their success demonstrates how the Cardinals' talent development process takes less-talented minor league players, and makes them into major-league caliber contributors.

The Cardinals' player development system aligns with the mindset, "All there is at work, is time to get better." Like any baseball team, the Cardinals make sure there is plenty of practice time. It's their job. But the Cardinals' process even establishes routines for engaging in pre-game practice. Go to any game in the Cardinal system. You won't see players clowning around or absent-mindedly going through the motions. Meticulous practice shows up in batting practice, shagging fly balls, and pitchers warming up in the bullpen.

Once a game begins, Cardinal coaches help players learn from their immediate game experience. As pitchers rest in the dugout between innings, a pitching coach debriefs the last inning to analyze what pitches were thrown, where (in plate location), and when (in the batting count). At the major league level, hitting coaches review videotapes of a hitter's earlier at-bats to pass along tips for their next plate appearance. Players inform teammates about an opposing pitcher's location and pitch command. These practices are now a habit.

Finally, the Cardinal coaching staff puts priority on instilling a meticulous player development approach over any deviation done for the sake of immediate, but fleeting, results. Putting process excellence ahead of an upsurge of results that can't be maintained, applies both to individual players' performance as well as a team's statistical performance. John Vuch points to this priority in this e-mail excerpt he sent to me:

> Over the long run, more success will be had by the player who consistently has a good approach, so we track "Quality at-bats" for our hitters, rather than just looking at batting average or on-base percentage. While we certainly use statistics in our analysis of our players, over the short-term those statistics can be impacted by a few hard-hit line drives being caught for outs, or conversely, some weakly hit balls may find a hole, or bloop over the infielder's head for a hit. We strive for the consistent "Quality AB." While it's sometimes tough to convince a player who hits two or three line drives directly at an infielder that he actually had a good game, they do understand we're paying as much or more attention to *how* they're doing it rather than just the results.

The coaching staff realizes players using a proper hitting approach during an at-bat are also establishing habitual movements and judgments needed to replicate stellar performance over the course of a season. On an organizational scale, the right player development approach pays off in decades of winning games and championships.

Business leaders easily relate to the Cardinals' strategy. They would love to staff a management team of A-players, while not having to pay humongous salaries. Unfortunately, a baseball team's approach does not directly translate as a talent development process for an office, manufacturing, or retail setting. However, it's possible to extract these three best principles used by the Cardinals to make your company one where all there is at work, is time to get better.

Best principle 1: There is a right way to perform the array of basic tasks required for the key positions on a team.

The Cardinal coaching staff goes to extraordinary lengths to explain the right way to perform the specific positions in baseball at all levels of the organization, from rookie league to major leagues. Spelling out performance standards for baseball players is similar to breaking down the facets of leadership in a business.

However, most companies employ a rigorous standard for front-line employees, and less-stringent ones for middle-to-senior managers. Front-line employees must comply with thick manuals to guide them when they're servicing customers or performing operational duties. But top leaders get a pass when it comes to refining basics. They are presumed to have learned from experience—largely from trial-and-error practice, or by observing their boss perform basic tasks. There's no quality control process to ensure such experiences lead to mastery of leadership skills.

To address this deficiency, the best-of-the-best talent development firms compile and publish a list of leadership basics, like decision-making, problem-solving, running meetings, or on-the-job training. Managers treat this list as a tool to weed out free-form basics. It makes it easier to spot a task being performed in a doing-what's-comfortable style, and, if necessary, define a step-by-step sanctioned approach for all managers to follow.

Best principle 2: There's a right way to practice to master leadership basics.

Very few baseball players turn out like the Seattle Mariners' Ken Griffey, Jr. and the Washington Nationals' Bryce Harper, who transitioned from high school to the majors with only a short stint in the minor leagues. Similarly, very few natural-born leaders can take charge of a team after just a few leadership training programs, developmental assignments, and mentoring sessions. Never underestimate the sheer amount of time and practice it takes to become an elite leader. The developmental path for leaders is filled with plateaus where the only way to attain higher proficiency is to discover better ways to practice. Just like the Cardinals, elite leaders bring intense mindfulness to their practice efforts, and to making the most out of job-imbedded development routines.

Best principle 3: The right priority requires placing process ahead of immediate outcome.

The Cardinals believe that perpetual success comes from teaching the best way of playing the game, and developing a player's talents to his full performance potential. But talent is always changing. Today's all-star becomes tomorrow's aging veteran. The Cardinals' strategy balances choices to drive winning now and stocking a pipeline of talent 3-5 years ahead.

It's definitely a counterintuitive notion to believe sticking to a process of continually refining basics will result in a winning season year after year. But great sports dynasties share one thing in common: their legendary coaches conceive a coherent, mindfully designed player development process, which they might fine-tune but from which they never deviate.

In business, senior management teams who cultivate talent development regard learning goals for developing elite leaders as the pivotal underpinning to drive sustainable winning results. In these remarkable companies, *learning* goals to prepare future leaders take the same, if not higher, importance as *doing* goals to deliver near-term results.

Most business leaders would find it a stretch to commit to best principles 1 and 2. But living up to principle 3 appears to be an insurmountable obstacle. How many CEOs can you point to who clearly declare their faith in a leadership development process as the basis to ensure consistent competitive advantage? It would be considered a hard-to-fathom degree of tedious activity if a business used the slavish precision similar to the Cardinals' meticulous approach in a business's leadership development process. Better to accept the customary leadership development trade-off, and forego this leap of faith strategy.

What might be called a leap of faith is really a mindset shift that brings with it make-or-break stakes. Isn't it time to break away from your competitors, those who accept merely competent leaders? Are you ready to discover what it takes to win with leadership development as the basis of your competitive advantage? If you're willing to orchestrate an eminent leadership development process, you could produce record-setting results, attract great employees, and competitor-proof your business. To see how it's done, let's study a case example of a fast-food restaurant chain led by a mindset master.

Pal's Sudden Service: Winning the Baldridge Quality Award in the fast-food industry

Pal's Sudden Service, a 22-store fast food chain based in Kingsport, Tennessee, has not only produced unprecedented results for its industry, but has won the Malcolm Baldridge Total Quality Award in 2004. Most Baldridge winners are manufacturers who originate *best practices* like total quality management and lean manufacturing. It's unprecedented for a fast-food chain to undertake the rigorous Baldridge application process, let alone win the award. When I dug deeper, I found that Pal's leadership development process drives their accomplishments.

In preparing for their first Baldridge contest, Pal's CEO Thom Crosby recalled a seminal mindset shift. "We realized we were screwed up from day one. We thought we were in the service business. We were wrong. We're serving three different functions, in this order of priorities. First, we're a manufacturing firm since we prepare our meals quickly and accurately, like an assembly line at Ford, converting raw materials into a car. Second, we're an educational institution that certifies our people to perform their jobs. Third, we're in the hospitality industry based on how we treat customers."[12]

By viewing fast-food as an integrated trio of industries, Pal's outperforms its competition. As a manufacturer, Pal's order speed is 20 seconds, compared to the fast-food industry average of 76 seconds. On the service side, complaints, usually about order accuracy, are a miniscule 4 per 10,000 transactions. On the education side, Pal's turnover rate among managers is .4 of 1% compared to the average for fast food chains of 4.7%.

Pal's widespread ability to outperform industry standards stems from rigorous selection of managers, as well as ongoing training and certification. Pal's senior managers' mindset about leadership development stands out among other fast-food operators who feel high turnover rates make it unreasonable to spend time in quality training efforts. Thom Crosby maintains, "Most organizations are obsessed with efficiency, and unknowingly drive themselves into the ground. Companies need to be efficient and effective. You need world-class players in leadership positions. When you have the right leaders in place, you have a true competitive advantage seen in the P&L. The monetary impact is sustainable and predictable."[13]

Pal's growth rate directly depends on the chain's capacity to develop qualified leaders. No restaurant opens until a general manager builds a skill set worthy of leading a crew that is capable of producing $2 million in sales per year from their 11,000 square-foot restaurant. Like the Cardinals and other talent development hotbeds, Pal's puts priority on long-term success. Properly educated general managers meet prerequisites for running a restaurant, which takes precedent over short-lived infusions of sales growth from additional stores.

From the start, Pal's sets the bar high by recruiting college graduates. The college recruiters are the general managers who give talks on campuses about Pal's business model and opportunities to grow as a leader. During recruiting trips, general managers practice public speaking skills.

For their first six months of employment, management prospects work as crew members (even scrubbing dumpsters and cleaning toilets) to learn the roles they might one day be supervising. At the same time, these candidates also participate in 12-20 mentoring sessions with CEO Thom Crosby, where they learn the values, standards, and process that have been used to produce powerful results during Pal's fifty years in business. The "Monday Mornings with Thom" training program gives general managers a chance to learn about the mindset of the Pal's past and present leaders. Crosby describes how historic decisions were reached, featuring intimate details of what ideas were tried and didn't work, plus the varied positions their leaders took on the issues. Candidates are assigned business books to read, and then they report on the lessons learned for managing at Pal's. They also keep a journal to gauge how their own emerging abilities stack up against their model of a world-class leader. Once they understand the company philosophy and best practices, each candidate conducts over two hundred restaurant inspections in six months. They identify gaps between the current operational effectiveness and Pal's elite standards, and suggest improvements to general managers. Restaurant inspections provide the trainees with plenty of practice in assessing restaurant operations and giving constructive feedback.

Once a candidate becomes a general manager, he or she conducts lots of on-the-job training for crew members. Stationed on the production line every day, she or he has specific goals about who to train, and what content or skills to be trained. Pal's doesn't have a single trainer on staff. Thom Crosby instills a mindset conducive to development: "To win, you have to out-execute. To out-execute, you have to out-train. It is a core part of our job. If you are going to be a world-class organization, you have to get onboard with training. It's just the reality."

Training and developmental opportunities occur as a coherent rhythm on a monthly and yearly time line. Thom Crosby, who spends 40 percent of his time in leadership development, delivers fourteen 2.5-hour leadership training sessions over each seven-month span. Every month, general managers join the three-person senior management team's steering committee to vote on key decisions. They apply Pal's beliefs and standards to describe the basis of their votes, and get feedback on their decision-making process. By putting decisions under the microscope, Pal's uses its own business as a case study to practice strategic thinking. Instead of annual performance appraisals, employees and managers receive quarterly developmental objectives, as well as semi-annual peer reviews. Every two years, managers take written tests for content knowledge, plus assessments of actual performance of basic skills.

At Pal's, the mindset, "All there is at work, is time to get better" is alive and well. There is no sign of a leadership development trade-off, even in an industry where time could easily be consumed by nearly non-stop customer transactions. As a mindset master, Thom Crosby orchestrates an experience where managers continually practice skills and meet prerequisites in order to take on greater leadership responsibilities.

Pal's talent development process is as intentional as The Cardinal Way. Pal's workplace is akin to a baseball practice field, where managers practice while conducting restaurant inspections, delivering on-the-job training, and analyzing their strategic decisions in steering committee meetings.

It's no coincidence the Cardinals and Pal's talent development methods share similar best principles for talent development. Like most sports teams, the Cardinals capitalize on learning from other fields, like sports nutrition, sports medicine, and sports analytics. Pal's breakthrough came from reconstituting their business as a mixture of a manufacturing firm, educational institution, and service agency. Having a mindset containing the best principles from disparate fields is the best catalyst for game-changer innovation, as you will see in the next chapter.

CHAPTER 03

GAME-CHANGING INNOVATION IN DEVELOPING LEADERSHIP TALENT

Michael Lewis, author of the bestsellers, *Moneyball* and *The Blind Side*, has captured the attention of a large audience by writing about innovators on Wall Street, in Silicon Valley, and in sports. In a *Fortune* magazine interview, he said: "I've seen over and over again in my subjects—and there is greatness in this—a trigger that goes off in their mind, a switch that flips when they sense that everyone is going one way, and it's stupid. And they take pleasure in taking a bloody-minded stance against it."[1]

One of Lewis' subjects, Billy Beane, General Manager of the Oakland A's, was a non-conformist, a game-changer in baseball. The sport would be very different today if he had not dared to challenge the prevailing mindset of the day. Thomas Edison, Sam Walton, Jack Welch, and Steve Jobs all went against the grain because they were willing to test an unconventional solution others either had not seen, or didn't dare to follow.

Any leader who aspires to deliver a game-changer innovation eventually discovers there is no choice but to generate an uncommon vantage point, one which makes it possible to conceive unique solutions, and to produce unprecedented results. These results transcend an industry's expected performance standards and alter the basis of competition.

Accordingly, benchmarking a trendsetter's well-established practices is only a start. Game-changer innovation requires discovering novel solutions to leap ahead of what's already known and being done.

> *For game-changers, there is no blueprint to*
> *benchmark, only the freedom of the page yet*
> *to be written.*

The pivotal question for an aspiring game-changer is where to look for a unique vantage point to spark innovation. If sports employ a world-class talent development process, then it's precisely the field for adapting liberating models, mind-expanding beliefs, and innovative practices for developing an all-star leadership team. Business can ill afford to continue treating sports as merely a source for colorful analogies.

In this chapter, I invite you to take a stand against conventional wisdom, and commit to breaking away from your competition. First, we'll examine the reasons businesses need to view sports as the preferred source for conceiving bold innovations in leadership development. Second, we'll investigate an essential mindset shift to drive game-changing innovation. This shift involves replacing benchmarking to copy another company's best practice with distilling the best principles of a disparate field, and then adapting them to fit your specific organization. Third, we'll apply a two-step drill for translating sports teams' assumptions about talent development into imaginative practices for building the capabilities of an elite leadership team.

Why Sports is an Ideal Catalyst for Game-Changing Innovation in Business

After submitting an article to the editor of an international publication on leadership, I received this feedback: "As a matter of personal prejudice based on long experience, I tend to reject articles about sports or the military. Business is a different context, with similar but different rules. It's like Newtonian physics and quantum physics."

Conventional thinkers, whose heels are planted firmly in the status quo, will point toward obvious differences. Sports accentuate physical skills, while business emphasizes thinking and communication skills. Since the players' performance during games is the essential product of sports teams, there aren't a lot of other priorities competing for time. Besides performing minor administrative duties and a post-game press conference, 100 percent of a coach's time is allocated to help players get better. Coaches can allocate substantially more time for practice to improve performance than managers can in business. Given these dramatic and obvious differences, conventional thinkers miss out on the profound catalytic value of connecting the player development process in sports to the realities of a hectic workplace.

I believe these common assumptions around talent development in sports are misperceptions that doom companies to produce merely competent leaders, now and forever. Why not break with conventional wisdom and consider sports champions as a source of best principles to convert into your own best practices for developing exceptional leaders? Let's look at these seemingly disparate fields through a different lens.

Performance in sports takes much more than physical skills

From a seat in the stands, sports fans observe just the physical movement of the players on the field. But that's only a partial view of athletic performance. Besides physical movement, athletes use thinking and communication skills in their gameday performance, such as:

- Decision-making in the heat of competition.
- Focusing attention and eliminating distractions.
- Communicating with teammates and coaches to ensure meticulous game plan execution.

In addition, preparing for athletic competition involves:

- Creative thinking skills while crafting innovative game plans.
- Taking responsibility for maintaining a mindset of unwavering confidence over a long season.
- Understanding the game plan so well that improvisational moves are performed flawlessly in the midst of competition.

These essential thinking and communication skills for athletic performance are also relevant to being a successful business leader.

Sports coaches face serious constraints on practice time

It's a mistake to assume sports teams have a massive amount of time to devote to player development. Sports-governing bodies, like the National Collegiate Athletic Association and National Football League, limit in-season and off-season practice hours when players can interact with coaches. However, the more substantial constraints on practice time come from considerations about the athletes' ability to perform at their peak. Coaches must design a practice schedule to prevent injuries, fatigue, and psychological burnout. They vary practice intensity so well-rested players can deliver their peak performance during games.

In addition, sports teams have limited time to operate as an intact group. Team rosters turn over 25-50 percent of players each year due to college graduations, retirements, injuries, and trades. Sports have well-defined seasons, so months go by when coaching staffs and athletes don't practice as a team.

Imagine what it would be like for you as a manager if 25-50 percent of your organization's employees were turning over annually, *and* the entire enterprise shut down for months of vacation. How would you cultivate continual performance improvement with those substantial diversions?

Sports teams depend on elite talent development to achieve business success

Sports are the ultimate pay-for-performance business. Their product isn't a high-tech digital device, fuel-efficient automobile, insurance plan, or high-carbohydrate energy bar. Customers pay to be entertained by players' performances in competitive games. In product development terms, each player's genetic talent is the raw material. The technique of physical movement, mental skills, and sport-specific knowledge acquired in the player development process all contribute to the finished product. Consequently, the coaching staff's full-time role is to develop its players' physical, emotional, and mental abilities—individually, and in a coordinated team effort.

As a business entity, any sports team composed of competent players will usually lose to rivals with superior talent. Talent procurement and development produces winning. Winning performance translates to increased revenue from game attendance, advertising, team merchandise, and media broadcast rights. There is one notable exception—the Chicago Cubs. (How does a team go over 100 years without winning a championship... even by chance?)

Talent development is clearly job one, the highest priority, for sports teams. As a business, they are best in the world at developing their talent.

Sports teams take an interdisciplinary approach to drive performance breakthroughs

Sports teams collaborate with other disciplines in a relentless commitment to improve performance. Coaches cross over the boundaries of other fields to adapt highly specialized expertise into their player development process. Demand for continual improvement in the player development process has created entirely new disciplines, such as: sports medicine, sports analytics, sports technology, sports science, sports psychology, and sports nutrition.

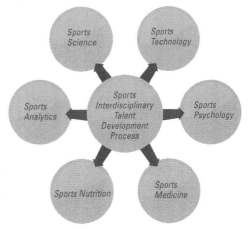

Elite athletic performance takes into account all of the disciplines needed to cultivate an athlete's full capabilities, as well as lengthen the average career. Let's look at a couple of examples where sports teams apply specialized knowledge from a variety of areas.

Sports nutrition is a relatively new science, which aims to provide an extra competitive advantage. At Stanford University's Arrillaga Family Dining Commons, dietitians code menu items for their beneficial effects on sports performance, brain performance, post workout recovery, and enhanced immunity. Chefs will toss anti-inflammatory ingredients such as thyme and turmeric into a dish to shorten a person's recovery time after workouts and injuries. They serve grass-fed beef, which has more omega-3 fatty acids than grain-fed beef, in order to promote heart health and immune response. As players select foods, information cards tout the health implications of various items. At the performance breakfast bar, Stanford athletes can sprinkle walnuts on their oatmeal while also scanning a research study citing that walnuts contain more antioxidants than any other nut.[2]

Can you fathom a conversation going on in your senior management team regarding the performance-enhancing qualities of food in your office cafeteria? Without a sports performance lens, no one would even bring up the subject.

Sports science studies the application of scientific principles and techniques, with the aim of improving sporting performance—incorporating areas of physiology, kinesiology, motor control, and biomechanics. As an example, sports scientists focus on recovery after, or in the midst of, a sporting event. Within twenty minutes after a swimming competition, camera feeds from above and below the water are gathered, with the data compiled and fed to coaches and swimmers in the cool-down area. Three minutes after Michael Phelps raced at the 2012 Olympics, when lactic acid associated with muscle fatigue is at its highest, a lab tech pricked his ear with a needle, and the blood analysis indicated the amount of millimoles of muscular waste that needed to be cleared from his system. Phelps gently did recovery swims in a cool-down pool until the readings dropped to acceptable levels, so his body chemistry was precisely calibrated for a peak performance in the next race.[3]

What if your company's IT staff devised a software program to do energy tracking so the team's workloads don't overwhelm individuals and cause substandard performance? Without a sports performance mindset, the notion of recovery doesn't get taken into account in business. More likely, employees are expected to recover from the daily grind of work when they get home after work or on weekends.

If I asked you to find a similar scale of talent development breakthroughs in business, you'd be hard-pressed to come up with examples. Ask yourself:

- How much has performance appraisal changed in the past thirty years?
- Is online learning an efficiency ploy, or a superior way to train certain basic leadership skills?
- Do 360-degree anonymous peer reviews boost performance dramatically, or discourage candor among team members?
- If everyone laments the difficulty of transferring training from classroom to the workplace, why is there no original, standout approach for following up training?

The Game-Changer Mindset Shift

The limits of innovation based on benchmarking

Where would you send your top executives and learning professionals to leverage innovative methods for leadership development? You might think the best place would be to study talent hotbeds whose best practices come field-tested from your own industry, and then take them wholesale to incorporate into your business. This practice, known as *benchmarking,* is common.

However, there is a hard-to-detect downside to benchmarking, especially within your own field or industry. It's likely that even an industry trendsetter's best practices were invented within a set of limiting assumptions about leadership development. These limiting beliefs assume:

- *There are only a few stars.* Assuming the normal distribution of leadership talent, the best you can hope for is to have a few extremely accomplished and below-average performers, with an overwhelming percentage doing a competent job. A goal of 100 percent elite leaders sounds far-fetched.
- *The most efficient way to convey learning is by lecture.* Give trainees what-to-do tips, and they'll be able to apply them in work situations.
- *You can only expect an accelerated learning curve in the first 12-18 months in a new role.* Learning rates never approach this intensity in

the later stages of a career. So lighten up on your expectations for steady improvement by veteran managers or long-time occupants of a role.

- *Performance plateaus are inevitable.* Managers eventually reach their optimal talent—sooner rather than later.

- *Job descriptions are etched in stone.* Once performance standards are written, they usually are good for at least a decade or two.

- *Infrequent feedback is expected and acceptable.* The bulk of performance-based feedback comes during performance reviews and 360-degree peer reviews.

- *You staff a business for the primary reason of controlling labor costs.* With streamlined staffing, it's not efficient to be sending people to training or spending time in developmental coaching.

- *You can't expect your managers to be stalwart trainers and coaches too.* Managers come from backgrounds in specific technical expertise like marketing, operations, and finance. They can't all be expected to function as training and development experts. After all, that's HR's job.

- *Acquiring basic leadership skills comes with experience.* Experience is a great teacher. Senior managers can be expected to have mastered most of the basic leadership skills.

- *Development requires the boss to be present.* The leader of a team provides the coaching, on-the-job training, and mentoring that are the prime occasions for leadership development.

These assumptions get treated as unwavering business realities. Accordingly, all emerging best practices will be watered down, compared to innovations free of these limitations.

If you aspire to develop 100 percent elite leaders, you need to stop treating these assumptions as ironclad rules which restrict what's possible in building leadership capabilities. In the pursuit of game-changer innovation, you're better off looking for bold ideas for leadership development from a different field that doesn't recognize these artificial constraints. You need to choose to make a mindset shift regarding the source of your innovations as displayed in the following figure.

Figure 3.1 — The Game-Changer Mindset Shift

From Customary Mindset of Competent Performance	To Transformational Mindset of Elite Performance
Innovation comes from benchmarking best-in-classes trendsetters, preferably from a similar industry.	Innovation comes from adapting best principles and practices from a disparate field—like sports.

Intersections as the breeding ground for game-changer innovation

In his book, *The Medici Effect*, Frans Johansson describes how trailblazing innovators conceive big ideas by being immersed in the intersection of disparate fields. He defines an *intersection* as a place where ideas from different fields and cultures meet and collide, ultimately igniting an explosion of extraordinary discoveries.[4] To generate innovation for leadership development, business leaders must cross over artificial boundaries between fields to seek original principles, practices, and questions that spark creativity.

Among the intersections involving sports and other fields, sports analytics has exerted enormous influence in the past decade. The first notable game-changer was Billy Beane, cited earlier in the chapter for his bold nonconformity. Beane was the first among baseball's front office establishment to embrace an unconventional innovation—a decision-making tool to alter talent appraisal as well as game management. The behind-the-scenes innovator in baseball analytics was Bill James, whose first "research laboratory" was a factory in Lawrence, Kansas. As a night watchman, he guarded the pork and beans. James had special talent in the field of analytics, which involves the discovery and communication of meaningful patterns in data. James' number-crunching approach, which he called *sabermetrics*, digs into baseball's raw data to examine long-standing traditional assumptions for appraising a player's contributions to winning games. His unique statistical analysis repeatedly proved that the following baseball traditions were a questionable basis for decision-making when compared to empirical data:

Tradition: The best way to evaluate pitchers is by their win-loss record.
Data: Pitching excellence is best measured by strikeouts, walks, and home runs allowed.

Tradition: The primary statistics to predict runs scored are a hitter's batting average and extra base hits.
Data: Players who get lots of walks and wear down pitchers are overlooked as contributors to run production.

Tradition: Sacrifice bunts to move runners into scoring position increase run production.
Data: Sacrifice bunts aren't worth an out when it comes to run production.

Tradition: Save your best relief pitcher, your closer, until the ninth inning when your team is ahead by a slim margin.
Data: Call for the top reliever at a game's turning point, even if it comes before the ninth inning.

Tradition: High school players who show promise at an early age possess greater upside potential, and are more likely to become the game's next superstars.
Data: College players are a better investment than high school players by a huge margin.

Tradition: Certain players are clutch hitters who perform better with runners in scoring position, or in a post-season championship series.
Data: There's little evidence that over the course of their careers, players exhibit better performance in clutch situations.

The term "tradition," is baseball's long-standing assumptions about selecting players and game strategy that are currently accepted, but not necessarily accurate. Billy Beane broke with baseball's establishment and traditions because he had no other choice. In running a small market team, he desperately needed a solution because he operated with a tight budget for player salaries and could not buy expensive talent. Beane embraced sabermetrics-driven talent appraisal to uncover undervalued players who could contribute to winning games without commanding superstar salaries. Gradually, on-the-field managers used data to make decisions like batting orders, pitching moves, and positioning fielders. More small-market teams became early proponents of sabermetrics. Even the Boston Red Sox, a team carrying substantial salaries, hired Bill James as Senior Advisor on Baseball Operations, and won three World Series. The most dramatic impact of this game-changer innovation comes in the last tradition-versus-data comparison:

Tradition: People who haven't played baseball can't help in selecting talent.
Data: The number of non-playing baseball general managers and analysts has increased every year since 2002. (Or put another way: If you want a job in sports, they're hiring geeks.)

As his game-changer innovation evolved into the new normal in baseball, Bill James rejoiced, "It is a wonderful thing to know that you are right and the world is wrong. Would God that I might have that feeling again before I die."[5] Right now, you have a similar opportunity to conceive extraordinary innovations by finding the vantage point where the player development process of sports teams intersects with leadership development in your business.

Game-changing innovation requires a unique vantage point.

Mindset Disturbance #3

Be ruthlessly honest. Ask yourself these questions to master the innovation mindset shift:

1. What relevance do you see for studying the field of sports as a way of promoting your team's fresh thinking about leadership development?

2. If your organization has relied on benchmarking best practices to drive innovation, how will you go about influencing your colleagues to study disparate fields like sports, performing arts, or military combat preparation?

3. What assumptions about leadership development are harming your company's ability to produce elite leaders?

4. How are you going to assemble a variety of unique perspectives to spark unconventional thinking and bold innovation?

Translating the Sports Performance Mindset Into Business Innovations

How much experience does your senior management team and human resource staff have in conceiving work-process innovations to build leadership capabilities? If you're being ruthlessly honest, the predictable answer is "None." Most companies have systematic processes for product innovation and marketing innovation. Inventing new, unique work process innovations, especially ones geared to cultivate leadership talent, is extremely rare.

To adapt ideas from disparate fields takes intersectional thinking. My favorite drill has two steps. First, keep a log of the assumptions that sports teams hold about player development. These assumptions might come from reading *Sports Illustrated* or *ESPN The Magazine*, hearing post-game interviews with players and coaches, or taking lessons with a coaching professional (golf coach, tennis coach, personal trainer). Then ask, "If business leaders believed the assumptions that sports coaches take for granted, how might leadership development look?"

The following sets of charts illustrate how the well established assumptions of the sports performance mindset might be translated into novel leadership development practices.

Figure 3.2a — Converting sports teams' customary assumptions into novel practices in business

Assumptions of Sports Teams About Practice	Imagine: If A Business Did This...?
Practice is an occasion where individual players improve their abilities, and team execution is perfected.	Managers design staff meetings with opportunities to practice basic leadership skills
Practices and games are videotaped for players and coaches to study.	Team meetings get videotaped. Time is allocated to study edited footage to improve skill proficiency.
Ritualized warm-up drills focus attention on giving a peak performance once the game begins.	Each morning starts with a warm-up drill where everyone practices setting learning goals to be accomplished during their daily activities.
Coaches instantly correct mistakes in physical techniques and mental errors, allowing players to immediately practice better methods and keep from ingraining bad habits.	Everyone expects to get feedback in public, especially around ineffective behaviors and bad habits. After receiving corrective feedback, people immediately practice more skillful responses with their teammates.
Teams select players based largely on how they actually perform in games and in practice.	Hiring goes beyond interviews to include opportunities to observe an applicant's skill proficiency and capacity for learning. Trial hiring periods are used for front-line positions.

The second chart adapts the prevailing assumptions in the sports mindset into innovative coaching practices in business.

Figure 3.2b — Converting sports teams' best principles into novel coaching practices in business

The Sports Mindset About Coaching	The Sports Mindset About Coaching
Sports teams have an operations' staff to handle non-coaching responsibilities. Coaching requires a full time role devoted to player development.	Staffing calls for two kinds of managers. One manager focuses on accomplishing operational plans, and the other manager emphasizes coaching to develop a team's capabilities.
Performance plateaus are temporary.	Managers customize practice drills for team members to decrease the time spent in performance plateaus.
Coaches who are experts in a particular sport, collaborate with specialists from other fields (e.g., sports nutritionist, sports psychologist, sport analytics experts, and strength coaches) to develop players' capabilities.	Businesses augment their managers' expertise with outside specialists (psychologists, wellness experts) as well as in-house experts in specific fundamentals (e.g., strategic thinking coach, trainer of mentors, public speaking coach, listening coach, mindset coach, meeting design coach).
Player development takes into account the whole person—physical, mental, and emotional capacities.	Leader development includes a) physical conditioning to produce the raw energy and optimal brain functioning that constitutes peak performance; b) mindset mastery coaching to generate a perspective conducive to elite performance; and c) emotional intelligence training to foster emotional balance in dealing with favorable and unfavorable circumstances.

The ideas contained in the "Imagine if a business did this..." column represent extreme departures from customary leadership development practices, concepts which aren't going to be discovered by simply benchmarking other businesses. Intersectional thinking requires the extra effort that sets apart game-changer innovation from copycat, benchmark-driven practices.

Business leaders who are willing to shift their mindset and look to sports teams as innovation catalysts will discover abundant solutions to the fundamental problem of time—finding time to get work done and time to develop leaders. And when you solve that dilemma, you change the game.

CHAPTER 04

TAKING ACCOUNTABILITY FOR YOUR MINDSET

What determines the upper limits of performance? If you ask a coach who develops athletes and a business leader who wants to improve an employee's performance, you get different answers. The equation for player development in sports looks like this: *Performance = talent + practice + mindset.* Specifically, coaching-up athletes' performance requires rethinking their practice regimen and disturbing their mindset. In contrast, the thinking about talent development in business substantially adheres to the equation: *Performance = talent + knowledge.* Managers believe the most efficient way to significantly improve performance is to provide their staff with more and more know-how. They are unlikely to orchestrate a new skill practice regimen or provide coaching aimed to cause a mindset disturbance. These equations illustrate the vast difference in the preferred approach each field uses to help employees realize their full performance capacity.

Consider the task of coaching a team member to master a performance plateau. In sports, a coach changes the practice regimen in a way that not only builds skill proficiency but also boosts a player's confidence. Because their beliefs about what they can accomplish change, athletes experience a mindset shift that transfers to game day performance. In business, a manager's first instinct is to provide plateaued employees with more training. But what happens when team members know what to do, but they don't just do it? What happens when their professional development requires doing things outside their comfort zone? The next response for most managers is to hold their direct reports accountable for not improving their performance, but they do it in a way that rarely works to master plateaus.

Although many companies proclaim accountability as a core value, the typical conversation around this important topic covers only observable, external factors—decisions, actions, and results. Everyone is accountable for their decisions, their actions, and their measureable results. Meanwhile, mindset, the vantage point that actually determines our decisions, actions, and results, remains missing from the conversation. Consequently, most performance management, accountability checks, and leadership development initiatives don't take into account the role that mindset plays in being root cause for determining the upper limits of performance, far more than the knowledge of tactics or how-to steps for executing skills.

Mindset disturbances, and the resulting shifts in the way we filter our experience, are the catalyst to freedom. They expand our choices so we can apply our knowledge and access our untapped capacity for leadership. Every employee's journey to becoming an elite performer involves generating mindset shifts to continually master performance plateaus.

It doesn't matter where you have plateaued—as a competent contributor, an elite performer for your company, or a world-class leader in your field—you must disturb the mindset that got you to your current level of performance to have any hope of moving to the next level.

In this chapter, we will explore how having an awareness of your mindset, and then employing specific steps to take accountability for it, ignites breakthroughs towards becoming an elite performer. You will be learning to raise your game as a leader by becoming a mindset master.

What You and LeBron James Have in Common

In a 2013 interview with *ESPN The Magazine*, LeBron James reveals what he termed "one of my biggest obstacles": "I'm afraid of failure. I want to succeed so bad that I become afraid of failing."[1] From our vantage point as sports fans observing his career unfold, it's nearly impossible to imagine James, the highly acclaimed, award-winning championship basketball player for the Miami Heat, is afraid of failing. LeBron James gained national acclaim in high school as experts proclaimed that his ideal raw talent made him likely to become the next Michael Jordan. Fear is not something we can see, or even imagine would be part of his thinking. But James' comments reveal he lacks the supreme confidence we assumed he had, and that he is not immune to fear.

Despite enormous natural ability, James played seven years as the marquee player for the Cleveland Cavaliers without winning a single NBA Championship. Basketball experts believed his championship drought would surely end if James had better teammates. They believed the solution was to change the external circumstances, not his internal mindset.

In 2011, James qualified as a free agent, and became part of the Miami Heat, joining fellow superstars and Olympians, Dwayne Wade and Chris Bosh. The Heat became an instant favorite to win a string of championships. Unfortunately, James played badly in the must-win playoff games. Although surrounded by talent, he could not optimize his own talents, and even more important, James fell short of delivering the caliber of leadership needed to win championships.

In 2012, James' name was finally taken off the infamous list of superstars who have never won a championship. Miami won an NBA title. James won an Olympic gold medal with the U.S. Men's Basketball team in London. In 2013, the Heat repeated as NBA champions.

What was the previously missing ingredient that sparked LeBron James' newfound capacity for winning? James and the Miami Heat coaching staff each generated mindset shifts. In combination, these mindset shifts led to the discovery of novel ways to exploit both LeBron James' vast array of talent and his emergence as a leader.

Let's look back to understand the role mindset shifts have played in James' evolving leadership role. In 2011, James announced his decision to move to Miami on a highly promoted, over-the-top primetime television special on ESPN. He drew sharp criticism from fans and media from around the country. As the crowds booed, James' face had an angry frown instead of his usual playful grin. He wasn't aware of it at the time, but he had adopted what he later called "the villain mindset." James explained in a 2013 *SI.com* story, "I lost touch with who I was as a basketball player and a person. I got caught up in everything that was going on around me, and I felt like I had to prove something to people, and I don't know why. Everything was tight, stressed."[2]

James' breakthrough as a leader of championship teams began when he reframed his mindset so the game was not an occasion to gain revenge, but for expressing his jubilance for playing basketball. He told himself: "This is what you love to do, and you've been doing it at a high level for a long time, and you don't really need to change anything. Just get back to what you do and how you play, smiling all the time and trying to dominate at the highest level. Do it with joy and do it with fun and remember that not too long ago this was a dream for you. Playing in the NBA was the dream. Don't forget that again. Just go out and improve."[3]

Meanwhile, the Miami Heat coaching staff was also undergoing their own mindset disturbance. They asked themselves, in what areas does the best basketball player on the planet look to improve? Dribbling? Rebounding? Jump-shot accuracy? The Miami Heat coaching staff didn't settle for these obvious answers. They also shifted their collective mindset, and reinvented the team's game plan to remove the previous restrictions—of fitting James into the five traditional offensive roles on a basketball team. In 2011, James played within the confines of being a small forward. In 2012, he essentially became position-less on the offensive end of the court. The coaching staff redesigned the playbook to take advantage of James' diverse skills as a contributor to point production, regardless of his position. When LeBron is introduced at a game, the announcer roars: "Number 6, LeBron James." That's all. No position is given.

With increased freedom to take charge, James altered his mindset to see himself as an all-court threat. "People tell me how big I am, but I don't see it," James insists. "I just remember that little freshman, taking the ball off the backboard and running. I'm a perimeter guy. Moving into the paint represented more than a new role. It demanded a new identity."

Miami Heat Head Coach Eric Spoelstra gave the entire team copies of the book *Mindset* by Carol Dweck. "What you're seeing now is marked improvement from the shoulders up," Spoelstra said. "For him (James) to have a historic year last year and to find a way to reinvent himself and improve, that speaks to his character and what's inside him." When asked to speculate about James' upside potential, Coach Spoelstra remarked, "We don't want to put a ceiling so I actually have never tried to put a limit on where he can be. He's in the physical prime of his career. But with his attitude and his commitment to a growth mindset, who knows how much better he can be?"[4]

What do you have in common with LeBron James? Obviously, I'm not suggesting you compare your caliber of basketball skill with his unparalleled performance. The common ground lies in galvanizing the most powerful ingredient in mastering plateaus at any level of performance—mindset. *You must disturb the mindset that got you to competent performance in order to become elite.*

Just like LeBron James, whether you're aiming to create a single behavior change or raise an array of skills to elite proficiency standards, the most important thing you can do is to take accountability for your mindset. And in doing so, you shift from the fear of being found incompetent to seeing the valuable learning that comes from trying, making mistakes, and even failing. That is how fear turns into confidence, maybe even pride, from accomplishing something that at times seemed impossible.

Moving from a Victim Mindset to an Accountability Mindset

Your freedom is at stake

Failing to take accountability limits your freedom to consider and act on any courses of action outside your comfort zone. During an executive coaching session with Walter, a CEO for a newly formed and fast-growing commercial real estate firm, he told me, "We can't embark on a new initiative to develop leaders right now. My managers tell me they're consumed with establishing the technology infrastructure, as well as the basic blocking and tackling of a startup business." Walter does not notice he is making a paralyzing assumption—that under startup conditions, a leadership team can't simultaneously execute both short- and long-term goals.

On the surface, the right-conditions-aren't-in-place card always sounds pragmatic and quite astute. However, as long as his team lays the technology infrastructure but neglects developing leaders, his organization has no coherent culture or work process. Do you sense there is an accident waiting to happen in this scenario? When the days reserved for laying down the technology infrastructure run out, Walter and company have no consistent caliber of leadership among the regional offices. Unfortunately, when Walter blames the pressures of a startup business, he is actually choosing to undermine his leadership team's ability to maintain a dual focus on short- and long-term goals—now and for the foreseeable future.

In sharp contrast, taking accountability for your mindset expands your freedom. At the end of my daylong seminars, I invite participants to describe the mindset disturbances they've generated, plus the powerful ways of expressing their leadership capacity that are now available to them. Paulette, a superintendent for a city government agency, said, "I assumed when I hit a plateau, it was evidence of my lack of talent." Every time Paulette stops improving, or struggles initially to change a behavior, she'll instantly chalk it up to a supposed lack of talent, making it unlikely she could expect to get much better as a leader. After engaging in exercises for taking accountability, Paulette describes her mindset shift, "Now I realize most plateaus have little to do with lack of talent, but can be mastered with the right kind and right amount of practice." Paulette can disregard a seemingly insurmountable obstacle—lack of talent—for the rest of her career. She will test first to see if flaws in her practice regimen are the real cause of her struggle to improve her skills. Paulette's mindset shift leaves her with an expanded freedom to pursue continual learning and professional development.

These two examples illustrate the destiny-shaping consequences associated with taking accountability for your mindset. Without a mindset shift, Walter's leadership team will never develop the capacity to manage short-term and long-term goals simultaneously. In contrast, Paulette's mindset shift enables her to stop blaming lack of talent as the cause of performance plateaus and to start a practice regimen to keep getting better.

Healthy disregard for the unreasonable: An accountability framework for mindset masters

Mindset masters are fully aware of the huge stakes associated with tolerating blaming or taking accountability. Accordingly, they employ a unique and empowering mindset about accountability, which has three key aspects:

1. *Accountability requires zero tolerance for blaming other people or circumstances.* To accept accountability means to discard the self-deception of portraying yourself as a victim of unreasonable circumstances that make it impossible to perform any better. Zero tolerance does not mean never blaming anyone or anything for the rest of your career. It refers to always catching yourself and shortening the time consumed in a blaming rant. Five days spent consumed with blaming compresses to a fifty-minute outburst, and eventually to five seconds.

2. *Accountability is a proactive, forward-thinking distinction, not an after-the-fact post mortem.* It requires being proactive in owning the circumstances. If the circumstances conducive to producing successful outcomes are not in place, an accountable leader takes actions to orchestrate the right circumstances. Accountability is something people step forward to accept, not avoid.

3. *Accountability reveals unflattering truths in a way that expands freedom of choice.* Accountability is a process of telling the unvarnished truth to yourself (or a coach) about your role in sabotaging results you claim to want. You reveal your choice to take actions that undermine your desired results, and then justify doing so to derive immediate payoffs. It takes courage to take accountability for your ineffective choices, and to see yourself as the source of your own diminished results.

As truth replaces self-deception, unreasonable effort and risk cease to be barriers, even coming to be regarded as wimpy or laughable. You find you can make new choices, even if only to test the supposed severity of obstacles you anticipate. Essentially, *you shift your power from being a victim with no say in the matter (other than blaming presumed limits) to being the cause of the results you produce (when you recognize you're the one fabricating a self-limiting mindset).*

President James Garfield captured the conflicting nature of accountability when he said, "The truth shall set you free, but first it will make you miserable."[5]

In my seminars, I share a framework for harnessing the power released from taking accountability for your mindset. The following diagram illustrates a continuum of reasonableness. It depicts our mindset as a series of subjective thresholds for determining the ease or difficulty in making behavior changes or pursuing results. By subjective thresholds, I mean regarding mindset as a fabrication, something made up—definitely not factual or based in reality. In addition, the space labeled "impossible" represents actions or results that are actually impossible for an individual to perform or accomplish.

Figure 4.1 — Healthy Disregard for the Unreasonable

Impossible

Unreasonable

Reasonable

Increasing Risk
Increasing Effort

This threshold for gauging reasonableness accounts for two variables: 1) the presumed effort involved in making a behavior change, and 2) the risks associated with failure to achieve desired outcomes. When we judge our effort and risk to make a behavior change to be reasonable, we feel confident and take consistent action. When we define a threshold to be unreasonable, any attempt to improve stops, and undermining behaviors, such as blaming, kick in. We don't even try to attempt behavior changes we've deemed to be impossible.

The lost opportunity comes when we mistake the threshold for "unreasonable" with "impossible." We easily concoct unexamined justifications that behavior changes are impossible when we have sufficient ability, or could eventually become capable. We could also choose to expend unreasonable effort or risk to achieve a worthwhile goal.

> *As victims, we create a charade that there is*
> *really no choice but to cave in to unreasonable*
> *obstacles. As a mindset master, we acknowledge*
> *we have a choice to expand our sense of what*
> *conditions constitute unreasonable effort and*
> *risk.*

In taking accountability for our mindset, we can display healthy disregard for the unreasonable. "Healthy disregard" refers to viewing the circumstances and available choices objectively and rationally, rather than through the self-limiting distortions brought about by a victim mentality. If you boil healthy disregard for the unreasonable down to core beliefs, it amounts to:

> *Mindset is an interpretive bias, a fabrication.*
> *Elite performers make a habit of discarding*
> *fictitious difficulties.*

Elite performers are mindset masters who seize the opportunity to rethink their criteria for what constitutes unreasonable effort and risk. By displaying healthy disregard for the unreasonable, they gain access into hidden reserves of performance capacity.

How mindset masters exercise healthy disregard for the unreasonable

To become a mindset master, you will need plenty of practice listening to your own self-limiting beliefs in order to develop a sharp awareness of your mindset—so you can use it as a force for igniting a behavior change. It is common for the blaming generated by a victim mindset to go undetected, even by well-intentioned and highly skilled coaches.

Let's examine four examples of blaming to illustrate how mindset masters take accountability, and reveal the unvarnished truth about self-deceptions that usually go unnoticed.

Blaming an unfavorable condition
"*My team has plenty of experienced employees nearing retirement, and they don't want to change.*" This justification is a dressed-up version of "You can't teach an old dog new tricks." It's a great excuse to cover up a manager's failure or hide our unwillingness to adapt training and coaching methods to motivate seasoned employees. It really says, "I am unwilling to change."

Accepting an unpleasant emotional state as an excuse
"*After several years of success, people grow complacent.*" This one is really clever. This story blames winning as the cause for failing to improve. Notice how easy it is to treat complacency as a natural emotional state that invariably accompanies success. Do you sense the "of course" or "without question" which underlies the diagnosis of complacency? Why can't past success kindle the desire to keep repeating success?

Blaming bad timing as an excuse to play it safe
"*That's a great idea, but there's so much uncertainty in the marketplace and in government policies. The timing isn't right.*" On the surface, this justification passes for senior management's astute reading of marketplace conditions—which could be true. But the same reasoning could also be a way to deflect accountability for

refusing to make proactive decisions to alter the competitive landscape. Besides, there's a false premise operating here—that the only appropriate time to change is when a market place is stable. Leaders can't produce enduring success unless they're earnestly contemplating how to execute great ideas under all marketplace conditions.

Blaming genetic or personality flaws for failure to change

"This is who I am, and you can't expect me to be someone I'm not." Steve Jobs actually offered this explanation for the rough edges of his personality to his biographer Walter Issacson.[6] This all-purpose justification, which blames his genetics, excuses any interpersonal flaw. He is a victim who lacks any power to change, and doesn't have to be responsible for his behavior.

Without sensitive listening, all of these vintage blames appear to be totally justified. Each captures the prototypical victim stance: "I'd change how I'm acting if only the required effort weren't so unreasonable, and the risks could be removed." Unfortunately, *most of us are well-practiced in blaming, and under-practiced in taking accountability for our mindset.*

Grasping the distinction between blaming and taking accountability for your mindset on an intellectual level is a start, but it's not enough. When you interact in a hectic environment where blaming runs rampant, your intellectual understanding will not make a difference. It takes plenty of practice for you to become proficient at taking accountability for your mindset. The best practice regimen takes this complex skill and breaks it down into concrete steps.

Five Steps for Taking Accountability for Your Mindset

Before laying out the five steps for taking accountability for your mindset, I need to prepare you for a radical departure from the typical coaching protocol. Here's my note of caution before you read any further.

> *The typical ways we hold people accountable increase blaming!*

Imagine we're eavesdropping on a team of managers' attempts to hold individuals accountable for missed results, or for being stuck at a performance plateau. We're likely to hear the following salvo of questions:

What happened that prevented you from achieving your goals?

What got in the way of your improving on the weaknesses we covered in last year's performance appraisal?

What caused you to miss the deadline?

Why didn't the result we planned for get accomplished?

Sound familiar? How do these questions prompt people to respond? They call for explanations, rationalizations, justifications, maybe even spinning and storytelling, which are all forms of blaming. *Managers think they're holding direct reports accountable when they're actually asking blaming-enhancement questions.* None of these blaming-enhancement questions take people to a deeper level of self-awareness needed to confront their constraint-filled mindset, which has everything to do with how we perform each of our tasks every day.

With this cautionary warning, you can proceed to replace blaming-enhancement questions with the following five steps for taking accountability for your mindset. Give yourself a beginner's mindset by engaging with the steps as if you know nothing about coaching to instill accountability.

Step 1: Describe the performance improvement goal or plateau you intend to master

A performance plateau occurs when an individual stops improving in any of three areas: 1) quality of skill proficiency; 2) range of capabilities; and 3) quantifiable business results. So the first step in plateau mastery is describing a performance improvement goal in concrete and measureable terms. Basically, you ask yourself the question, "What will it look like to master this plateau?"

In your answer, consider the following four ways you can change behavior and ask yourself this series of questions:

- **To stop** ineffective behaviors, ask:

  What bad habits do I know I need to curtail?

  What are the automatic efficiency measures or low-priority tasks that I use to escape facing a challenging task where my competence is sure be tested?

  What is the strength responsible for my past success that I rely on too much, which actually undermines my ability to achieve my current goals?

- **To start doing** effective behaviors which expand capabilities, ask:

  To deliver on my new responsibilities or expected results, what new skill would be worth developing?

  What new behavior/skill set will I need to learn and start doing if I want to add more value in my interactions with my internal and external customers?

- **To improve proficiency** in performing specific tasks and skill sets, ask:

  What would it look like to move from a scripted, step-by-step training protocol proficiency to a more spontaneous skill proficiency?

  What improvisation can I experiment with during my upcoming opportunities to perform this task?

  How can I improve the quality of performing a task by choosing a particular intention, such as being compassionate, playful, inquisitive, authentic, or meticulous?

- **To increase frequency/time allocation, ask:**

  What behavior do I need to attempt more frequently or spend more time on to deliver the results I want?

  What's the difference between the time I allocate to key tasks comprising my job, compared to the time spent by elite performers in the same role?

In your answers, describe a specific behavior or combination of behaviors. For example, the answer, "Improve coaching skills to an elite standard," is too vague. A better answer would be, "Stop asking blaming-enhancement questions, and start asking questions which invite people to take accountability for the choices they make that contribute to unwanted outcomes."

Step 2: Identify self-induced barriers brought about by your choices

Taking accountability enables you to gain insight into the self-induced barriers that block your ability to upgrade your performance. Self-induced barriers consist of a chain of three ineffective choices emerging from the victim mindset: undermining behaviors, justifications, and hidden short-term payoffs.

Be ruthlessly honest in answering this next set of questions. They may seem a bit unsettling to confront because you will be required to face unflattering truths, and you'll find no wiggle room for justifying a lack of results. These accountability-oriented questions will help you expose your own choices to take the easy way out—to forgo your desired results in favor of short-term comfort. Ask yourself these accountability-driven questions in the following sequence:

1. *What actions have I chosen to take or to avoid that undermine my efforts at behavior change?*

2. *What difficulties or justifications do I choose to accept as valid reasons for not accomplishing the performance improvement I want?*

3. *What are the short-term payoffs I choose to accept, even though they keep me from being able to perform better?*

Below is a list of common short-term payoffs:
- Avoid increased responsibility
- Avoid new problems
- Avoid raising expectations
- Avoid dependence on others for cooperation
- Avoid harder work
- Avoid more time demands
- Avoid losing nice-guy image
- Avoid stress
- Avoid having more to lose
- Avoid loss of relationships
- Avoid failure
- Avoid facing unpleasant truth
- Avoid being seen as incompetent
- Avoid loss of support
- Avoid losing control of decisions

What makes these short-terms payoffs so compelling that people are willing to forfeit any chance at a major accomplishment?

The strongest reward of all is preserving your identity—how you see yourself, and how you aspire to be seen. We identify with our roles, our desired reputations, our perceived competence, and our organization's stature. When our identity is threatened, we go into survival mode. Self-protection becomes mandatory, taking precedent over improving performance or accomplishing a vital goal. Preserving an identity is a survival issue. It is defended with the same intensity you'd expend to keep your job.

In my executive coaching, senior managers have expressed these unforgettable statements, which show the importance of preserving their identity at the cost of diminished results:

- "If I do my job and develop a team of outstanding technicians, I won't stand out as a star technician."

- "I have to be fake and phony and go along with the management team's majority position on most issues. Otherwise, I will stand out as a maverick, which isn't a good reputation to have in such a rule-bound organization. It's better to be considered a good team player."

- "I can't prepare for a meeting since I pride myself on being a guy who can think on his feet, which is more impressive than being a disciplined sap who does things by the book."

Would any of these expressions be embarrassing and hard to admit to yourself, let alone to your boss? These truths are meant to disturb your mindset. While they are hard to admit, digging deep and discovering these justifications is essential for replacing them with a more empowering mindset. Mindset disturbance is the precursor to freedom of choice.

Step 3: Declare a commitment

A moment of truth arrives when you must choose between two opposing commitments: 1) pursue the performance improvement goal in hopes of transcending a plateau, or 2) give up in order to gain a compelling, guaranteed, short-term payoff. At this point, the big questions get answered. Is your commitment to mastering a plateau merely a pipe dream? Or is pursuing your commitment to gain short-term payoffs a self-deception that's run its course? To clearly choose between opposing commitments, address this question:

> *Am I ready to give up the short-term payoffs in exchange for the opportunity to have the results I desire?*

Step 4: Test your lingering self-limiting beliefs through safe-to-fail experiments

If Step 3 doesn't reveal your true commitment, dig deeper. Step 4 is reserved for occasions when you're reluctant to commit to a behavior change until your prediction of unreasonable effort or risk is tested.

Safe-to-fail experiments confirm the accuracy or, more often, reveal the fallacy of our justifications. In the victim mindset, we treat the prediction of unfavorable outcomes as if they are 100 percent correct. However, a single incident where the unwanted outcome doesn't occur can instill doubt in the prediction's accuracy, which can mushroom into a full-blown mindset disturbance. A new sense of safety emerges from discovering a menacing prediction didn't actually happen. A seemingly far-fetched goal becomes totally doable.

The best safe-to-fail experiments are designed with a strong likelihood of achieving the desired outcome, while containing a manageable amount of stress. Ask yourself:

> *How can I test my expectations of unwanted outcomes so there's manageable discomfort, but not overwhelming stress?*

While working with Rebecca, I posed this question to begin designing a series of safe-to-fail experiments. Rebecca was a new member of a senior management team. Our coaching focused on her being forthright in expressing her own positions on controversial issues. Rebecca assumed being the youngest member of the team required her to earn credibility before her challenging, and sometimes opposing, opinions would be taken seriously. Rebecca imagined her more seasoned colleagues poking holes in her positions, leaving a terrible first impression. We constructed this progression of safe-to-fail experiments with each one carrying an increased risk:

- State your minority opinion in a one-on-one conversation with a senior manager who's been a past mentor, or has shown enthusiasm for your participation on the team.

- State your minority opinion with a team member you don't know well, but who's a good listener, open-minded, and unlikely to be threatened by the issue at stake.

- State your minority opinion in one-on-one interactions with the CEO.

- State your minority opinion with a team member who is liable to feel his or her self-interest threatened by your opinion.

- Deliver a formal presentation detailing your minority opinion before the entire senior management team.

Rebecca's goal in this series of safe-to-fail experiments was to see whether her original prediction of being viewed as lacking in strategic savvy came true. The actual result—whether or not her colleagues disagreed or agreed with her position—was secondary. Each time her prediction of diminished credibility with colleagues was proven false, her confidence for sharing her opinions with unfettered candor increased.

Step 5: Change your mindset so it's conducive to reaching your performance improvement goal

Rebecca discovered her fresh perspective was actually a valuable contribution that shook up the management team's deeply entrenched viewpoint on several pivotal issues. As a result, her mindset could incorporate a revised assumption: A newcomer's unbiased viewpoint is extremely valuable to a long-standing management team.

Every time you take accountability for your mindset, pause to appreciate the significance of your accomplishment. Acknowledge your courage in exercising healthy disregard for what appears to be unreasonable effort or risk. As a leader, whenever your freedom of choice expands, your direct reports' capacity for leadership grows as well. Since you've proven a self-limiting belief to be manageable, you will not consider it a source of unreasonable effort or risk when your team members mention it. You'll become much more effective in spotting victim language and inviting colleagues to take accountability for their own mindset.

Declare a Ban on Blaming

Vistage International is an executive coaching firm and network of peer advisory groups, sharing experiences to help one another improve their businesses. I enjoy presenting to these CEOs because they are quick learners, and have a thirst for actionable ideas to take back to their companies. Sometimes the groups apply the actionable ideas before my seminar is even over.

During one presentation, Jerry, CEO for a chain of drug stores, shared his strong reservations about his ability to stick with the formal structure and precise questions in the five steps for taking accountability for choices, actions, and mindset. His actual comment was, "I lack the self-discipline to stay with any kind of structured approach." I instantly said to the group, "Did you hear that wording? Does it sound like a victim mindset?" I left the podium, walked over to Jerry and said, "Do you really mean to suggest you have deficient genes or a permanent personality flaw?" I stayed silent, allowing time for the group to contemplate the destructive impact of a victim mindset. I then reframed it, "Jerry, could you say it more accurately, like 'In the past, when I've been given structured formats to follow, I haven't been reliable in choosing to execute the prescribed steps?'" Everyone heard the infusion of power when the wording shifted to recognize Jerry's personal choice in producing an outcome, even an unwanted outcome.

> *It makes logical sense. If you're the source*
> *of the problem, then you're also the best source*
> *for the solution.*

I repeated the same coaching drill when I heard participants offer justifications like, "You get dragged into the minutia," suggesting this is a widespread, unavoidable incident, and "I don't want to ruffle feathers," implying there's no way of communicating that won't upset a colleague. After observing my coaching, these CEOs started calling each other out for adopting a blaming posture by asserting, "Mindset shift." The Vistage members took over my role as mindset master, and decided to install this ritual to ban blaming in their future monthly meetings.

Practice Drill: Calling Out Episodes of Blaming

Declare a ban on blaming for your management team. Executing the ban requires vigilant monitoring and deliberate practice in group interventions, self-coaching, and enlisting support from an accountability coach.

Take the ban public

Follow the model of the fast-learning Vistage CEOs. Invite your colleagues to practice detecting when any team member uses words indicating a victim mindset, by saying in an encouraging tone, "Mindset shift." Then team members must pause to allow the speaker to rephrase the victim-mindset language with new wording that takes accountability for his or her choices that undermine desired results. With practice, everyone's victim mindset sensors will become highly attuned to more empowering language.

Self-coaching

Practice catching yourself each time you launch into a blaming tirade. If you're working alone, stop to jot down the justification you use to excuse your undermining behavior. If you're involved in a conversation, stop talking momentarily and say, "I'm going to stop blaming now." Then practice taking accountability for your mindset by filling in these sentence stems:

1. I'm choosing to do (or avoid doing) _____, which keeps me from accomplishing my goals.

2. I'm choosing to justify my lack of results by claiming _____.

3. I'm choosing to accept the short-term payoff _____.

Get a coach who will stretch your mindset

You will get more out of this practice drill and the ones that follow by inviting coaching support from a colleague, an executive coach, a friend, or your spouse. Whoever you pick, choose someone who will stretch your comfort zone.

While learning any new sport requires stretching to make muscles more flexible, developing leadership abilities requires stretching one's mindset to gain access to hidden reserves of performance capacity. "Stretching" means expanding your sense of what constitutes unreasonable effort and risk when mastering a plateau, or making a challenging behavior change. Ask your coach to ask questions and occasionally offer feedback to help you engage in honest self-reflection and come up with the action plans called for in these practice drills.

Key takeaway idea

Each time you blame the practice drill for being tedious, hokey, or upsetting, remember what's at stake.

*Taking accountability for your mindset
determines the degree of freedom you'll have
available to express your capacity for leadership.*

CHAPTER 08

The Critical Role of Mindset Masters in Developing Leaders

In my decades of interacting with senior executives, a few individuals stand out by their extraordinary ability to take ideas they've heard in a speech, and implement them with robust results in their organization. In every case, these outliers emerged due to a mindset shift.

Andy Tysler is Vice President of Sales for Deschutes Brewery, based in Bend, Oregon. In the midst of a seminar discussion about the impact of mindset on performance, he came to the conclusion, "So if I as a leader, and by extension my organization, have the same mindset as everyone else in the industry, then we will end up being average." Weeks later in debriefing our coaching call, he described a mindset shift about his own leadership role in this e-mail:

> I've always believed in training my people, but my mindset shift calls for incorporating training and development as an everyday and even every sales call process. Training is not a once-in-a-while aspect of the job, it is an everyday aspect of the job. I'm no longer a sales manager offering up random training or offering coaching when a direct report makes a mistake. I'm a full-time developmental leader who's available to reinforce my team members' good habits, help them improve on poor habits, and discover their strengths and weaknesses.
>
> Another change brought about by my mindset shift involves letting trainees do a rigorous self-assessment after each sales call while keeping my mouth shut, so they debrief themselves with me present. If I do all the talking, it becomes me telling them. If I coach my team on how to debrief themselves, then they make more impactful discoveries and it reinforces their own habit of engaging in self-assessment.

Where does taking accountability for your mindset rank in the full arsenal of leadership skills? Leadership development programs emphasize three basic areas: interpersonal communication skills, technical skills, and cognitive skills. Little emphasis is placed on perceptual skills, which involves developing a capacity to understand how mindset impacts on a leader's choices and actions.

The role of mindset master is perhaps the most underappreciated and underdeveloped qualification for leadership.

Jeremy Hunter, an expert on mindfulness in the workplace for the Peter M. Drucker & Masatoshi Graduate School of Management, wrote this description of the value of perceptual skills: "When leaders apply an old map to a new problem, they find themselves stuck, stressed, and frustrated at their lack of progress."[7] Using Hunter's analogy, mindset disturbance means trashing an old map and drawing a new one, which is the precise role of a mindset master.

Perceptual skills are called for when leaders must escape from biases that prevent them from contemplating bold courses of action. There are two primary occasions where perceptual skills make a huge difference—innovation and coaching. Innovation calls for dispensing with the limits that have been imposed by conventional thinking in order to generate a new vantage point for conceiving novel solutions. Coaching for mastering plateaus requires an ability to expand the criteria for what constitutes unreasonable effort and risk.

I want you to fully appreciate what's at stake in your becoming a mindset master. Taking accountability for your mindset is the best method for tapping into your hidden reserves of capacity for leadership. You will enjoy profound satisfaction from knowing you're fully expressing your natural talent for being a leader. You will be free to pursue seemingly far-fetched goals and initiate actions that used to seem unreasonable. In being a leader who can distinguish mindset as a mental fabrication, rather than a formidable external roadblock, you will transform your ability to influence team members to take bold action.

Becoming a mindset master is the prerequisite for empowering competent leaders to become elite, and for elite leaders to become legendary. The next phase of the Leadership Development Game Plan involves developing a mindset and a skill set conducive to being a deliberate practitioner.

PHASE II:

PRACTICE LIKE A PRO

Leadership Development Game Plan

Phase I:
Generate the Mindset
of an Elite Performer

Leader's role:
Mindset Master

Phase II:
Practice Like a Pro

Leader's role:
Deliberate
Practitioner

Phase III:
Orchestrate the
Learning-While-Working
Process

Leader's role:
Orchestrator of
Elite Habits

CHAPTER 05

YOU'RE ALWAYS PRACTICING—FOR BETTER OR FOR WORSE

The phrase "Practice makes permanent," is attributed on several online quotation sites to UK soccer coach Bobby Robson. Robson's quote takes on far greater significance by adding five words: "For better or for worse."

In soccer and other sports, practice is revered and treated like a core competency. Coaches attend off-season clinics to learn the best practice methods. They compete among their coaching brethren to see who can devise a superior brand of practice. Players get drafted for multimillion-dollar contracts, in part based on their practice habits. They compete to play on the first string unit to get more quality repetitions of practice drills. Teams videotape practice, and then scrutinize the footage to use as a teaching tool with players. Everyone believes the way a team practices determines how well they play on game day.

Even in individual sports, practice is the undisputed key to gaining dominant competitive advantage. Coach Bob Bowman developed a recovery regimen that followed strenuous workouts so swimming icon Michael Phelps could practice one more day a week than other swimmers. At least fifty more workouts over a year helped to produce a nearly unbeatable edge in the Olympic Games. Track legend Edwin Moses studied physics and engineering at Morehouse College, and used his background to improvise his running mechanics. As architect of his own unique practice, Moses figured out how to take thirteen steps between hurdles in the 400-meter race, while other world-class hurdlers took fourteen steps. He never lost a single race in his athletic prime, which spanned over a decade.

Athletes and their coaches understand the implications of practice. The difference between being a top-flight competitor and being an all-time great might be the result of one more day of practice each week, or taking one less step between hurdles. Practice isn't neutral. Practice always makes a difference—for better or for worse.

Few business leaders attach the same destiny-shaping stakes to the frequency and quality of their practice. They permit practice to produce "for-worse" outcomes—either not improving their team members' skill proficiency, or actually reinforcing their bad habits.

How does this happen?

1. *Ineffective behaviors get practiced.* Team members are permitted to practice ineffective behaviors, like micromanaging, feigning real listening, multi-tasking, giving boring presentations, or blaming circumstances for missed results. There's no norm in place to call out a colleague for incompetent performance—when it happens. Instead, people take note of the ineffective behavior, so it becomes a topic of conversation during a peer 360 review, or in performance appraisals months later.

2. *Insufficient practice occurs during and following training.* Training programs intended to produce changes in behavior do not allow sufficient time to practice new skills and get feedback. Instead, they consist of a lecture followed by Q&A, with no time for skill practice. Upon returning to work, trainees feel unnatural using new approaches and are likely to quit practicing these new skills, and soon revert to their old comfortable ways of doing a task.

3. *Practice amounts to nothing more than going through the motions.* Most employees are unknowingly practicing to plateau. They do what comes naturally in performing daily tasks, without a clear intent to improve by engaging in more rigorous practice.

In summary, most businesses suffer from an impoverished, for-worse quality of practice.

There are good reasons for this widespread lack of appreciation and poor application of practice. Effective practice methods aren't taught in the standard curriculum in high school, college, business schools, corporate universities, or new-employee orientation training programs. You probably learned about practice through sports, perhaps in Little League baseball as a child, or taking golf lessons as an adult. On the job, your time was spent getting work done efficiently, and you rarely found time for practice. As you assume more leadership responsibility, your boss probably presumed you'd accumulated so much managerial experience you didn't need to practice basic leadership skills.

Here's the final challenge that's unknown to most leaders. You never were taught the value of translating athletes' practice methods into your daily work.

This chapter will address these gaps, and enable you to take the initial steps for mastering the second role in the Leadership Development Game Plan—becoming a deliberate practitioner. You will learn what behavioral science research has found out about the part natural talent, as well as proper practice, play in becoming an elite performer. With a heightened appreciation for the value of practice, you'll learn the essential steps of deliberate practice, which is the most time-efficient way to get better in performing any skill. Finally, you will come to notice there is no shortage of practice opportunities. In fact, you're always practicing. You will learn to practice consciously in order to capitalize on ever-present opportunities to improve your abilities, and to grasp new knowledge.

Why Talent is Overrated and Practice is Underrated

"We don't rise to our level of expectations. We fall to our level of practice."
  – Bruce Lee, martial arts champion

I once believed that two factors—innate talent + hard work—were the basis for gauging the upper limits of an individual's performance capacity. I couldn't conceive of any other factors. Can you? That was my mindset about the upper limits of performance capacity, and I never considered anything else. If you've reached the same obvious conclusion, you'll feel empathy for my wake-up call regarding the value of proper practice.

I was fortunate to be able to custom-tailor my job to suit what I liked to do, and could do well. And I couldn't conceive of working any harder. According to the Talent + Hard Work formula, I had reached my peak performance.

I was in for a rude awakening when I began reading an article, "What It Takes to Be Great," by Geoff Colvin in a 2006 issue of *Fortune*. Colvin shared insights from a massive body of research on becoming an expert or elite performer in fields like surgery, sports, chess, performing arts, writing, computer programming, firefighting, and aviation. This loosely organized group of researchers on expert performance examined statistics, biographical details, practice diaries, and results of laboratory simulations.

With my yellow highlighter, I marked the sentence, "*Talent has little or nothing to do with greatness.*" I thought, "That's preposterous!"[1]

The "little" part that talent plays in producing elite performers, particularly in jobs where physical abilities aren't consequential, involves two factors. Superior talent is an advantageous launching point for the pursuit of extraordinary achievement. Second, engaging in work that affords plenty of opportunities to express your talent is vital to becoming an elite performer.

However, talent alone doesn't guarantee smooth sailing to becoming an expert in a given field. Many genetically gifted individuals adopt short cuts, squander opportunities to improve, accept plateaus as upper limits to personal growth, and get intimidated by other talented individuals. The term "underachiever" describes people with abundant talent whose accomplishments don't measure up to less talented colleagues.

My pen was now poised as I closely scrutinized each sentence. Suddenly, the next mindset-altering gem appeared: "So greatness isn't handed to anyone, it requires a lot of hard work. Yet that isn't enough, since many people work hard for decades without approaching greatness or even getting better. What's missing? Deliberate practice."

Deliberate practice is an abrupt departure from the way most business people treat practice, which is as a warm-up, review, walk-through, or repetition of existing strengths. Dr. Anders Ericsson of Florida State University is the foremost expert on becoming an expert. He defines deliberate practice as "the engagement with full concentration in a training activity designed to improve a particular aspect of performance with immediate feedback, with opportunities for gradual refinement by repetition and problem-solving."[3]

In my communications with Dr. Ericsson, he validated my own definition:

> *Deliberate practice focuses on mastering tasks*
> *beyond one's current level of comfort and*
> *competence, with a relentless intent to improve*
> *skill proficiency and expand a repertoire of skills.*

Let's break down my definition of *deliberate practice* to appreciate what this daunting and remarkable undertaking actually calls for. Start with the phrase, "mastering tasks beyond one's level of comfort." This is not mindless practice or repeating existing strengths with very little conscious effort. When you consider whether to engage in a round of deliberate practice, you're likely to experience unpleasant emotions like loss of confidence, apprehension, fear, and even dread.

The second part of the definition is "mastering tasks beyond one's level of competence." *Deliberate practice* requires the willingness to repeatedly set stretch goals and embrace inevitable incompetence in the attempt to perform better. Elite performers don't have to look good while performing in front of peers or their boss. They aren't afraid to make mistakes. With each attempt to raise the bar, initial failure is likely, but they know failure is a precursor to incremental improvement.

> *Elite performers don't care about feeling*
> *comfortable or making mistakes.*
> *Getting better is what counts.*

How would you feel at the outset of a career knowing you would spend many hours engaging in tasks you don't feel like doing, and aren't particular good at? If you're being honest, you probably feel like my clients who anticipate the journey will be a grueling, intense ordeal. In the short-term, avoiding fear and failure sounds like a better way to spend your time.

What's the alternative to investing considerable hours in practice for many years? Without *deliberate practice*, your attempts to get better will be hit-or-miss. You'll eventually hit a plateau, and mistakenly conclude you've achieved peak performance. Over the span of your career, when you're asked to take on greater responsibility, you'll encounter more problems in developing sophisticated communication skills for wielding influence as a leader. Even worse, you will never act with the conviction and satisfaction of knowing you are expressing your absolute best effort in pursuing your dreams.

Dramatic improvement to qualify you as an elite leader requires many hours of deliberate practice. The only problem: any other way takes longer. Deliberate practice is the most efficient and research-tested way to improve performance, no matter what your baseline level is, or the level you aspire to reach.

By the time I finished the *Fortune* article, I knew my for-certain formula for success—peak performance being the combination of talent and hard work—had been proved to be wrong. Talent is overrated. Deliberate practice has a stronger influence on greatness. Hard work is imprecise. Deliberate practice is the form of hard work that produces constant improvement. I vividly recall saying to myself, "Deliberate practice, where have you been all my life? Say hallelujah!"

I was jubilant over this mindset disturbance.

> *I was no longer stuck in the inherently unanswerable question, "Have you reached your full potential and maximized your talent?" The more powerful and answerable questions is, "Has your deliberate practice been sufficient to meet your highest aspirations?"*

I want you to fully appreciate my epiphany. Whenever you think to yourself, "I may not have enough talent," stop and pay close attention to what you're really saying. Unless you've worked diligently at deliberate practice, you're making the wrong diagnosis, and making it too soon. Operating with a new mindset about the upper limits of performance, you can now make a course correction based on a more accurate premise, "I may not have been doing sufficient deliberate practice."

Why Perfect Practice Doesn't Make Perfect

Legendary football coach Vince Lombardi told his Green Bay Packers, "Practice does not make perfect. Only *perfect practice makes perfect.*" In hearing this statement, most people assume the word "perfect" refers to perfect performance of the specific skill being practiced. If you practice incorrectly, you're practicing to make errors. If you practice perfectly for your stage of skill development, you're improving.

That line of thinking oversimplifies the behavioral science research. The notion of perfect practice doesn't take into consideration how well an individual practices to achieve a standard of perfection for any single skill. It's more accurate to say perfect practice refers to only one skill set—deliberate practice—and its application to any type of physical, thinking, or communication skills. For whatever task you're practicing, there is only one right way to practice, and that is deliberately. So it's more accurate to say:

*Perfect **deliberate** practice makes perfect.*

To begin testing the quality of your practice efforts, start by checking to see if you've complied with these steps for deliberate practice:

Step 1: Set a long-term stretch goal, or elite standard of performance, for a particular skill.

Step 2: Describe a noticeable improvement in the skill where practice requires you to go out of your comfort zone and exercise strenuous mental concentration.

Step 3: Design practice situations so you can get feedback on the skill you're looking to improve. Feedback sources include:
- Review a video showing your performance.
- Assess your strengths and weaknesses while in the midst of performing.
- Arrange to receive feedback from your boss, team members, or even customers.
- Obtain measures of desired results expected from performing the skill.

Step 4: Set specific improvement goals for each successive round of practice, get feedback, and use it to improve.

Step 5: When you hit plateaus, either a) break down the practice step to be closer to your current skill proficiency, b) invent new practice drills, or c) increase the frequency of practice. You'll learn four practice methods to accelerate plateau mastery in Chapter 6.

To practice perfectly requires meticulously executing these five steps of deliberate practice for any skill you wish to improve. Let's describe perfect practice for one of the basic leadership skills that eludes most executives—listening. Ken, the managing partner in a law firm, is one of my favorite examples of designing a deliberate practice to steadily improve. By Ken's own admission, listening didn't come naturally to him. He often glanced at his iPhone to check for messages, or he'd interrupt with his opinions instead of allowing the firm's partners to finish their sentences. Unfortunately for Ken, ineffective listening had become an automatic habit.

To improve his listening, Ken decided to treat every team meeting and one-on-one conversation as his most important activity for any given moment. Simply by focusing his attention, Ken gained dozens of opportunities to practice listening every day, and hundreds within every month. I developed a three-stage practice regimen to help him upgrade his listening skills from incompetent to competent, and finally, to elite standards.

At the stage of incompetent listening, the practice drills were designed to help Ken be conscious enough to notice and stop negative behaviors. When he caught himself figuring out what to say next while he was listening to someone, he would stop the distracting thoughts and give himself the command, "Focus on hearing each word," and make the adjustment. Whenever Ken talked over someone, he would stop the conversation, apologize for the interruption, and invite his colleague to continue. Then Ken would return to being a fully present listener. Ken kept practicing until it became natural for him to be riveted to a colleague's every word.

In the next phase of competent listening, Ken practiced being able to accurately restate what he heard so his colleagues would feel understood. During practice drills, Ken would paraphrase his understanding of the speaker's just-completed remarks, summarize the gist of a longer conversation, or ask clarifying questions. Ken told his colleagues about his learning goal, and requested their help. He took time at the end of conversations to elicit their feedback on the accuracy and helpfulness of his paraphrases, summaries, and clarifying questions. Once again, Ken practiced the skills for competent listening until they became second-nature.

Finally, I raised the standards for Ken to master the skills of an elite listener, which requires going beyond conveying an accurate understanding of a colleagues' communications. His practice focused on two qualities:

1. *Empathic listening.* The listener acknowledges his understanding of how the speaker feels about a situation, especially if the emotion was only implied. Example: "You feel encouraged by your colleagues' feedback that recognizes noticeable improvement in your listening skills."

2. *Challenge self-limiting beliefs.* The listener helps a team member stop blaming, and start taking accountability for an unwanted outcome. Example: "You're describing your team as being too thin-skinned to be able to hear honest feedback on their weaknesses without becoming defensive. What actions have you chosen to take, or to avoid, that might contribute to your team's reluctance to hear this kind of feedback?"

Notice how a basic skill like listening gets broken down into a series of proficiencies, each with an increasing degree of difficulty. When a level of skill proficiency is mastered, it's time to raise the bar, and deliberately practice the next level, in order to eventually reach elite standards.

While this description of Ken's progress from incompetent to competent—and finally to elite—listening is accurate, it makes the process sound far too smooth. It omits his non-linear efforts to improve, which occur in all deliberate practice. Instead of perfectly practicing listening skills, most of Ken's practice was far from perfect.

Deliberate practice is not a simple matter of consistent improvements which eventually lead to being able to perform a skill to perfection. It's moments of progress scattered throughout a long period of time when Ken was making mistakes, but also relentlessly sticking with the steps of deliberate practice. Once

Ken perfected one facet of performance, then the bar was raised, and he returned to making mistakes and being imperfect—but at a higher level.

Now you see the fallacy in the "Perfect practice makes perfect" conventional wisdom. We mistake "perfect" to mean practicing at a high degree of proficiency for a particular skill set. If somehow your practice was always perfect by this standard, you'd be practicing to plateau at a new, more proficient performance level, but you're still stuck in a comfort zone. Once you settle into a comfort zone, you're no longer participating in deliberate practice to improve your performance.

You're Always Practicing—for Better or for Worse

Having a clear understanding of what constitutes *deliberate practice* is vital to becoming a deliberate practitioner. You get more adept at noticing the "for-worse" practice methods. You can embrace a vital mindset shift: *We're always practicing.*

> *Every minute we're at work is an occasion ripe for practice. The real issue isn't finding time to practice. We're already practicing. What matters is whether the type of practice leads to "for-worse" outcomes (including plateaus) or "for better" outcomes (towards mastery).*

How do you feel about this implication that every minute at work is spent in some form of practice? Disbelief? Disagreement? Puzzled? Enthusiastic agreement?

I don't expect you to agree instantly. But notice that right now as you ponder the validity of this provocative idea, you're engaged in practice. You might be practicing defensive listening to prove that you're right in assuming deliberate practice is impractical at work. Or you could be practicing open-minded scrutiny of the value of this counterintuitive idea. At this very moment, you can choose the style of listening—defensive or open-minded—you're going to practice.

CHAPTER 09

Practice Drill: Becoming Aware of How You're Practicing

This practice drill will help you grasp the pervasiveness of daily practice opportunities, and sharpen your ability to sense the "for-better-or-for-worse" quality of your practice.

Self-assessment of your practice habits

This questionnaire contains a series of paired behaviors. For each pair, circle the behavior that best describes how you spend most of your time practicing. Don't over-think this exercise. Go with your first response.

How do you spend most of your time?

Micromanaging by doing tasks yourself	OR	Developing others so you can delegate
Multitasking	OR	Focusing attention on the task at hand
Pursuing safe distractions	OR	Doing vital, but challenging activities
Staying out of trouble	OR	Bringing up emerging problems
Sucking up to your boss	OR	Sharing your original analysis of an issue
Blaming circumstances for poor results	OR	Taking accountability for poor results
"Winging it" when preparing for meetings	OR	Practicing skills when preparing for meetings
Engaging in small talk at conference breaks	OR	Collecting actionable ideas
Listening to talk radio during commute	OR	Listening to audio books on business
Engaging in tactical discussions	OR	Engaging in strategic conversations
Figuring-out-what-to-say-next listening	OR	Seeking-to-understand listening
Sticking to "how we've always done it"	OR	Rethinking work processes
Leaving a vague voice mail	OR	Leaving a compelling reason to call back
Filling your day with urgent priorities	OR	Pursuing vital-but-not-urgent priorities
Making fake I'll-get-back-to-you agreements	OR	Treating agreements as firm promises
Wearing your emotions on your sleeve	OR	Managing stress to display an upbeat tone
Delivering boilerplate sales presentations	OR	Customizing sales presentations

To gain valuable insights from this practice drill:

1. Review your circled items. The left-hand column of behaviors consists of "for-worse" forms of practice which undermine skill improvement. The right-hand column contains behaviors worthy of deliberate practice to develop leadership basics. In which column do you spend most of your time?

2. To excel at spotting ever-present practice occasions, keep adding your own examples of paired behaviors to my list. Notice when you're going through the motions of doing a task, instead of treating the occasion as a performance. Recognize when you "make work" to avoid practicing a more vital-but-challenging task.

This series of practice habits is the tip of the iceberg. To rate yourself, or employ this drill with team members, use the full inventory, which is downloadable at **www.turock.com.**

Key takeaway idea

Do you see how every moment at work is a form of practice? It's only a matter of what you're practicing. The assumption, "Deliberate practice is impractical," just isn't true.

Do you see that any moment you can be mindful of what skills—for undermining or for empowering skill development—you're practicing? And being mindful doesn't take any time. The assumption, "There's no time for deliberate practice," is also incorrect.

CHAPTER 05

Becoming a Deliberate Practitioner 1.0

In this chapter, you've established a solid foundation for being a deliberate practitioner. You can appreciate a clear-cut consequence—how you practice determines how fast your performance can improve. You are also prepared to approach every task as an occasion for deliberate practice. While you have a huge advantage over colleagues who practice lackadaisically, you are still quite limited.

You're a one-trick pony deliberate practitioner. You have only one move—to do more of the same deliberate practice.

I wish you could apply a single deliberate practice regimen, and continue to improve your expertise and abilities for an entire career. But, ultimately, you'll hit plateaus, and stop getting better with only one approach. You've maxed out on your capacity that is confined to a single deliberate practice method, not on your innate talent.

The next phase for becoming a deliberate practitioner involves learning the four methods of deliberate practice, which I identified by studying professional athletes who are elite deliberate practitioners. While each method conforms to the requirements of deliberate practice, certain ones work better for mastering a specific plateau or developing a new skill. As a deliberate practitioner, you will be able to select a single practice method or combine a couple to achieve your own performance improvement goals, and those of your team members. You're about to learn how to practice like a pro.

CHAPTER 06

THE POWER OF DELIBERATE PRACTICE

Nothing is Left to Chance

Dave Scott is the only six-time winner of the Hawaiian Triathlon. On an average training day, Dave rode his bike 75 miles, swam 20,000 meters, and ran 17 miles. Dave Scott wasn't totally satisfied with the advantage he had over opponents because of his volume of training, or capacity for quick physical recovery. He also believed a low-fat, high-carbohydrate diet would give him an extra edge. Even after burning 5,000 calories a day in training, Scott still rinsed his cottage cheese to get off the extra fat.

Lindsey Vonn, Olympic gold medalist in downhill skiing, takes extreme measures in selecting skis for competition. After working with a manufacturer to customize a ski model for her unique requirements, Vonn and her team ordered dozens of pairs, and then began testing to discover the absolute speediest pair in the batch. Due to any number of miniscule variations in manufacturing (e.g., varnish thickness), one pair turned out to be faster than all the rest.

Vonn trained six to eight hours a day, six days a week. In Austria, she bicycled on Tour de France-style hills up the Alps. Perhaps the most challenging gym exercise required her to balance on a tightrope in a squat position, while throwing a medicine ball against a wall at different angles.

In sports, plateaus are considered intolerable. Athletes and their coaches are deliberate practitioners at a world-class level. Practicing like a pro means no detail is too small to overlook in order to gain a potential performance edge—like draining cottage cheese or testing varnish thickness. Nothing is left to chance when it comes to getting better.

In business, plateaus are considered inevitable. After mastering a series of common, easily mastered plateaus, employees reach a point where their competent performance no longer gets better. Most managers mistakenly interpret a plateau as their team member's optimal performance. It's a damaging misdiagnosis. The possibility of expressing their full potential gets left to chance.

> *Are you ready to make the mindset shift from*
> *believing plateaus are inevitable to considering*
> *plateaus as intolerable? Are you ready to practice*
> *like a pro?*

Consider this chapter as a version of the course in Becoming a Deliberate Practitioner 2.0. This curriculum is tailored for anyone willing to be unreasonable, and to leave nothing to chance in designing a practice regimen to master performance plateaus.

There are two main reasons plateaus persist: 1) we are slow to recognize them; and 2) we are *unintentionally* practicing to plateau. Both of these performance management challenges are about to vanish for you and your team. You will learn a set of questions to use to identify hard-to-detect performance plateaus. By sharpening your awareness, you minimize time spent at a plateau. You will also replace ineffective practice habits with four deliberate practice methods used by top athletes and anyone who seeks to be an elite performer in their profession.

Figure 6.1 – Deliberate Practice Methods to Adopt

Deliberate Practice Methods to Adopt	Ineffective Practice Habits to Terminate
Getting great at high impact skills	Getting good at all the basic skills for a job
Performing with second-nature skill proficiency	Stagnating at follow-the-training protocol proficiency
Cross training using complimentary skills to fortify strengths	Repeating more of the same practice of existing strengths
Devising safe simulations to perform without fear	Avoiding fear-provoking situations that are critical to goal achievement

This chapter contains practice drills to instantly apply in your leadership role at work, at home, or in your community. Once you learn how to practice for continual improvement, plateaus become short-lived, and your upside leadership potential keeps getting redefined.

A Systematic Approach for Identifying Performance Plateaus

Practicing like a pro doesn't eliminate plateaus, but shortens their duration. The sooner a leader can recognize a plateau, the faster she or he can create a new practice regimen to transcend it. In sports, the performance measurements are easily quantifiable so plateaus are easy to spot. This isn't the case in business. If an individual performs competently, plateaus can go undetected for years.

In this next practice drill, I'll explain the tool I use to start coaching sessions with my clients. This tool precedes any actual coaching conversation. Hundreds of managers have employed this tool to identify hard-to-detect and hard-to-admit plateaus.

③ *Practice Drill: Questions for Recognizing Plateaus*

The sooner you can recognize a plateau, the quicker you can devise practice regimens to improve your skill proficiency and results. This practice drill will help you scan classic situations where plateaus typically occur for managers, such as: a) vital tasks for which there's never sufficient time, b) new skill sets necessary to prepare for greater responsibilities, and c) the strengths you rely upon too much which hinder your leadership development.

Recognize your own plateaus

Go through these six questions rapidly the first time. If you can't come up with an answer to a question, leave it and move on. Certain questions will trigger an immediate response. Write down the details to get the best results. Get ready to be surprised by some of your answers.

1. What vital tasks or activities are never given sufficient time to get done?

2. What crucial conversations have you avoided, or handled ineffectively, which are obstacles to achieving better results in the foreseeable future?

3. Consider your recent performance appraisals or 360 peer reviews. What ineffective behaviors do you need to change? What effective behaviors would you need to initiate to replace your ineffective behaviors?

4. In the next year, what new responsibilities will you likely be taking on? What plateaus do you need to master in order to excel in these new responsibilities?

5. On what strengths do you over-rely? When does using the strengths responsible for your past success undermine your power to produce the results you desire today?

6. What is one behavior change you can make to produce your desired results more efficiently, or make certain tasks unnecessary?

Go back and review your answers using the following code:

- Code any answer with a "G" to signify "gulp," when you feel anxiety at the prospect of mastering this particular plateau. You master a challenge to arrive at a certain plateau.

- Code the answer "H" to indicate "high impact" on your organization/ team's performance

The items coded with G and H will assume top-priority status when you choose plateaus to master through deliberate practice.

To make plateau recognition a standard procedure, repeat the previous set of questions and coding at the beginning of every quarter.

Make plateau recognition an occasion for teamwork

Invite team members to share their plateaus with the entire group. Encourage individuals to pair up with colleagues who have mastered a similar plateau. Everyone can benefit from the lessons their peers have learned.

Key takeaway idea

Elite performers regard plateaus as inevitable, but not tolerable.

Deliberate Practice Method 1: Getting Great at High-Impact Skills

Kobe Bryant is the favorite athlete of the Nike product developers who customize sneakers for superstars to endorse. In an interview with Bill Simmons on ESPN. com, author Malcolm Gladwell explains why Bryant is so popular.

> Why? Because he (Bryant) kept pushing them and pushing them to make the right shoes for him, even flying there for days at a time just to put himself through grueling workouts with sensors all over his body. This past summer, he pushed them to create a special low-top sneaker that also would prevent him from

rolling his ankles—which seems incongruous on paper—yet they feel as if they pulled it off. And only because he kept pushing them. Forty years ago? He's wearing crummy Chuck Taylors like everyone else.[2]

And it's not just the shoes. It's Bryant's deliberate practice regimen that makes him a basketball icon. He has spent much of his life developing extraordinary footwork, and going beyond every NBA team's standard athletic conditioning programs.

Of the broad array of basketball skills to choose from, why would Bryant focus on footwork? There's much more glamour in being a great shooter. No statistics are kept on the quality of players' footwork. This isn't soccer where players kick the ball and score goals with their feet.

According to James Gelles, writing for the website, Coach's Clip Board:

> Basketball is played on the fingertips and the balls of your feet. Everything you do involves correct footwork. Some players are naturally quicker than others. But a player's effective quickness can be greatly enhanced if he/she uses proper footwork. A naturally quick player who lacks good footwork skills can be beaten (or contained) by a player with sound footwork fundamentals.[2]

Footwork pays off in Kobe Bryant's unprecedented range of improvisational moves on the court. Defenders try to anticipate his moves, but Bryant will sense the direction they're headed, make the right pivot, and go the other way. Opponents leap in vain or stagger off-balance, while Bryant positions his body for the best angle to make a shot.

Bryant began developing his moves while playing soccer in Italy, where he spent part of his childhood while his father, Joe Bryant, played basketball.[3] As he matured, he studied video footage of the footwork of Charles Barkley and Michael Jordan. One summer, Bryant worked out with Hakeem Olajuwon, learning creative moves for scoring in the congested area close to the basket. Throughout his career, he's fanatically studied game film to prepare offensive moves that capitalize on superb footwork to counter opponents' defensive tendencies.

Keystone habits: An ideal place to identify high-impact skills

Focusing on getting great in specific high-impact skills goes against conventional performance management wisdom, which preaches the importance of being good at all the basics. Performance appraisal systems offer a comprehensive assessment of an employee's strengths and weaknesses relevant to their job. Most performance standards are given equal weight, so individuals don't know where to focus their deliberate practice.

How do you go about determining high-impact skills needed for your role at work? Charles Duhigg's book, *The Power of Habit*, describes the notion of "keystone habits." As Duhigg writes, "Keystone habits start a process that, over time, transforms everything. This, then, is the answer of where to start: focus on keystone habits, those patterns that, when they start to shift, dislodge and remake other habits."[4] A keystone habit produces ripple effects, which flow into other areas of your life. They're the epitome of high-impact skills.

As an example, public speaking is a keystone habit for many tasks involved in leadership development. Outside of formal speeches, leaders face plenty of occasions where they are called to deliver an influential message, such as:

- Giving succinct elevator speeches at networking events
- Describing product benefits or organizational capabilities in a sales presentation
- Eliciting buy-in to a large-scale change initiative
- Interviewing for a job or for a media appearance
- Handling a question-and-answer session
- Organizing ideas logically in a written strategic plan for the senior management team

Besides public speaking, my favorite keystone habits include taking accountability for your mindset, listening, giving feedback, prioritizing goals, and, of course, deliberate practice.

What is the most impactful keystone habit? Physical exercise deserves strong consideration. According to Dr. John Ratey in his book, *Spark: The Revolutionary New Science of Exercise and the Brain*,[5] exercise stimulates new brain cell growth, which leads to better capacity for processing new information and maintaining solid brain functioning with aging. Essentially, the brain works just like muscles in your arms and legs, growing with use, and weakening with inactivity. Regular exercise enhances thinking capacity by:

- Improving memory.
- Lengthening attention span.
- Boosting decision-making skills.
- Improving multitasking and planning.
- Maximizing learning capacity.

Besides neurological benefits to improve thinking, sticking with an exercise program requires practice of self-management skills such as declaring a commitment, goal setting, time management, and taking accountability for your mindset.

 ## Practice Drill: Identifying High-Impact Skills

In this practice drill, you will learn techniques to identify high-impact skills, and to upgrade your team's performance appraisal process to achieve optimal results.

Consult with your own in-house experts

Let's use the job of project manager to illustrate this four-step process for you to follow in identifying high-impact skills and the best on-the job practice methods:

1. Ask a group of project managers to brainstorm a list of primary tasks that comprise their role.

2. Invite the group to compose competent and elite performance standards for each task on the list.

3. Invite three or four elite project managers to review the list and identify the three most vital tasks which contribute to success in their roles.

4. Interview these elite performers to find out how they practice these three vital tasks.

Leverage keystone habits

Keystone habits, by definition, are high impact skills, because of their wide application in different areas of performance. Think creatively and add to the following list of keystone habits:

- Visualization
- Focusing attention
- Creating safe-to-fail experiments
- Taking accountability for your mindset
- Setting goals
- Physical exercise
- Public speaking
- Listening
- Giving feedback
- Writing
- Deliberate practice
- Allocating priorities
- Decision-making

Your additions:

Now choose a specific keystone habit from your list to concentrate on mastering for the next six-month period.

Focus on high-impact skills during quarterly performance appraisals

Don't tolerate unfocused performance appraisals where the implicit expectation is to shore up all your weaknesses and leverage all your strengths. Instead, divide the year-long appraisal process into focused quarters, during which only two or three high-impact skills get the largest amount of deliberate practice. At the end of the year, notice how concentration on high-impact skills delivers bigger results than spreading your performance improvement efforts over the full range of competencies for your job.

Key takeaway idea

Less is more. Concentrate performance improvement efforts on high-impact skills.

Deliberate Practice Method 2: Overlearning to Perform with Second-Nature Skill Proficiency

Raymond Berry, the Baltimore Colts wide receiver who was a 20th round draft pick, ended his career being inducted into the NFL Hall of Fame. He didn't start on his high school team until he was a senior, even though his father was the coach. In three seasons at Southern Methodist University, Berry caught only 33 passes before being selected by the Colts in the 20th round of the 1954 NFL draft.

Lacking physical gifts, what was Berry's secret to such phenomenal success? Mark Bowden describes one example of Berry's deliberate practice regimen during a solitary preseason workout in this excerpt from *The Best Game Ever*: [6]

> The tall skinny young man in glasses was playing an entire football game at the split end position in pantomime. He had chosen the film of a particular game, observed each route run by the wide receiver, timed each play and interval between plays with a stopwatch and, in tiny, meticulous handwriting, sketched the patterns and noted the sequences. Every play, whether the receiver was thrown the ball or not; every huddle; every timeout; every stretch the wideout spent on the bench between offensive series. Then, consulting this handwritten script out on the grass, he acted out the game from whistle to whistle.

Forget calisthenics! Raymond Berry's offseason conditioning program was designed to be in "game shape" at the start of fall practice. He wasn't just physically fit, but was also ready to run passing routes with exquisite precision.

During the season, Berry scrutinized game films to detect opponents' vulnerabilities, and he collaborated with quarterback Johnny Unitas to introduce precision-timed pass routes, instead of depending on a pass receiver's sheer speed to get open. They perfected an exact timing for plays so the pass receiver would reach a precise location on the field just as the pass arrived from the quarterback. Raymond Berry's unique style of deliberate practice enabled him to reinvent the wide receiver position.

A primary job for coaches of athletic teams is to figure out how to get performance requirements ingrained in muscle memory. For instance, Don Shula, the winningest coach in NFL history and co-author, with Dr. Ken Blanchard, of *The Little Book of Coaching*, says, "Perfection happens only when the mechanics are automatic and overlearning is the only way to make that happen."[7] Coaches realize their players must get lots of repetition in practice drills to improve coordination with teammates, so everyone fulfills their assignment on a particular play.

Replacing stick-to-the-training protocol proficiency with second-nature skill proficiency

Second-nature skill proficiency refers to an acquired, deeply ingrained habit that gets done automatically, without requiring conscious thought about the steps to take. The performance occurs naturally because the task itself has been done so many times before.

How many managers have you worked for who insisted that you overlearn a task to reach second-nature skill proficiency? More likely, a stick-to-the-training protocol proficiency gets a pass. A "paint-by-the-numbers" phase in initial skill development becomes accepted as competent performance.

But relying on a scripted protocol ensures the performance never looks natural, polished, or spontaneous. Think of managers who've been trained in listening skills, and still use stilted training sentence stems like, "What I hear you saying is… " Think of restaurant servers who recite the same lines to guests, like, "Can I get you started with a drink before your meal?" Anyone who slavishly adheres to a training protocol has no chance of being fully present to the emerging experience when it might be better to improvise.

Overlearning to reach second-nature skill proficiency frees your mind to dream up new moves in the midst of everyday events. For instance, once you're highly proficient at inviting individuals to take accountability for their mindset, you can spontaneously inject this approach while your entire team does accountability checks to debrief a just-completed project. During a networking event, you might introduce a teachable moment, where you model your well-honed elevator speech for a colleague. After each demonstration, your colleague describes the effective elements of your content and style of delivery, and then practices his own elevator speech.

Even more important, second-nature proficiency is required when things aren't going according to plan. Imagine receiving a complaint from an irate customer whose purchases constitute 25 percent of your company's annual revenues. This unexpected complaint is not the time to adhere to the meeting agenda, which suddenly is no longer pertinent. Checking your memory for "the five steps to defuse angry customers" is not only too slow, but will likely come across as inauthentic. Instead, you rise to the occasion by demonstrating authentic caring for the customer's concerns, and then conceive an impromptu recovery response to exceed their expectations.

Practice Drill: Functioning With Second-Nature Skill Proficiency

In this practice drill, you will select vital skill sets you rarely get to practice. You will also learn to customize your own developmental assignment while staying in your current job. The overall goal is to increase your opportunities to practice particular skills.

Orchestrating practice repetitions in your daily activities

1. Compile a list of tasks where you are not performing with second-nature skill proficiency; areas where you still rely on memory crutches or step-by-step formulas. In addition, add skills you may be deliberately neglecting to practice, thereby compromising your effectiveness.

2. Create practice routines to use in regularly occurring situations so you get plenty of practice. For instance, set a goal to deliver performance-based feedback to at least three direct reports every day. Focus your intention on eliminating stock phrases for giving feedback that your team learned in a recent training program. Plan to weed out any vague words and insert precise descriptions of behavior which cover the three core elements of feedback—a) identify the skill category you're observing, b) specify strengths and weaknesses in the performance, and c) suggest areas for improvement.

3. Revise meeting formats to correct poor skill execution. For example, imagine that a number of your managers make decisions based on short-term considerations while totally ignoring long-term implications. To raise their awareness of this shortcoming, use the weekly team meeting to review big decisions pending for the month and repeatedly ask the primary decision-makers questions like:

    -   What long-term considerations do you need to take into account?"

    -   If you decide to take this course of action to improve this year's profits, what emerging future opportunities may be compromised or get missed entirely?

    -   By not choosing to pursue the potential long-term initiative, are you making assumptions that your team members are not able to deliver a sufficient return on investment?

By repeating these questions, your team members will quickly catch on and automatically raise the same long-term considerations when they make decisions.

Customize your own developmental assignment

Let's say you want to improve your ability to lead without having formal authority. Your developmental assignment could include any of the following activities:

- Arrange and facilitate a peer accountability group with your trade association colleagues who want to maximize their take-home value from the association's annual meeting.

- Present a well-researched counterproposal to your boss on an issue where you'd like to see him, or her, adopt a different solution.

- Champion a cross-functional task force to solve a recurring problem, and

- Form an ad-hoc group for the purpose of staging a recovery response to address a dissatisfied customer's needs.

Key takeaway idea

Never underestimate the importance of repetition of leadership basics. Design your own work process, as well as team meetings to incorporate the frequent skill practice necessary to shape and master second-nature skill proficiencies.

Deliberate Practice Method 3: Cross Training Using Complementary Skills

To transcend the point of diminishing returns from repeating the same practice drills, top athletes employ cross training to improve performance in their sport. For instance, football is seen as a predominantly strength-centric activity. Yet certain skill positions require flexibility, speed, agility, focus, and balance. Where do these skill players get the cross training to develop those facets of performance?

Hall of Fame wide receiver Lynn Swann of the Pittsburgh Steelers credits his graceful performance on the gridiron to ballet training. Swann was known for his exquisite body control, balance, sense of rhythm, and the timing of his movements, even in midair leaps. In an article, "What Ballet Does for Football,"

John Casteele of Demand Media[8] points to the cross-training benefits that aren't derived from football's typical weight training regimen and practice field drills. For a wide receiver, ballet helps with:

- Flexibility for making the body twists and contortions needed to outmaneuver a defensive back and make the catch
- Strengthening legs without adding unnecessary muscular bulk
- Balance for making acrobatic leaps to catch the ball without losing footing, and staying on their feet while defensive players try to tackle them
- Mental focus for simultaneously tracking a thrown ball in the air, as well as the approaching defenders, to quickly decide the best position to make a catch

The business equivalent of cross training

To design your own cross training regimen, first identify a strength that's no longer improving, and then survey complementary skills, which might be practiced in combination to uplevel your performance.

In considering cross-training options, select from these five categories of complementary competencies:

1. *Technical skills* such as software programming, marketing data analysis, and writing technical procedures.

2. *Communication skills* including empathy, open-minded listening, influencing, assertiveness, confronting discrepancies, public speaking, performance-based feedback, raising issues, and negotiating.

3. *Thinking skills* covering major categories like describing facts, logical reasoning, decision-making, judging, intuition, and idea-generation.

4. *Energy management skills* encompassing sleep, nutrition, hydration, stress management, and exercise.

5. *Self-management skills* including goal setting, time management, identifying plateaus, and deliberate practice.

As an example, Thomas is a CEO who is already a captivating and persuasive presenter. He realizes soliciting casual feedback from a few colleagues after a boardroom speech eventually produces modest gains in helping improve his speaking skills. Big advances are more likely to come from cross-training activities to build complementary skills like:

- Taking an acting course to get comfortable injecting the captivating impact of nonverbal behaviors like gestures, silence, and vocal variety to engage an audience.

- Developing the complementary skill of storytelling by listening to audio books of fictional story collections to grasp the structure for creating compelling drama while delivering poignant lessons.

- Studying tapes of TED presentations (www.ted.com) to learn a broad range of delivery techniques. TED presentations are categorized by qualities like fascinating, ingenious, inspiring, funny, and informative.

- Attending meetings of the advertising department to learn a variety of ways to word attention-grabbing and persuasive messages to move people to take action.

6 Practice Drill: Cross Training to Leverage Existing Strengths

A well-conceived cross-training program will dramatically accelerate your professional development. To deploy your strengths more powerfully through cross-training, you and your team can engage in the following practice drill, one which calls for using complimentary skills.

Design your own cross-training program

To identify a plateau requiring cross-training, ask yourself:

- What new responsibilities am I taking on, where relying only on my well-honed strengths will undermine my future success?

- Which of my leadership strengths show no signs of improvement due to my current deliberate practice becoming stale?

- How can I improve several complementary skills to fortify my existing strength?

Then design a cross-training regimen using the five categories of complementary competencies noted previously: technical skills, energy management practices, communications skills, self-management skills, and thinking skills.

Peer coaching

Practice developmental coaching with a colleague who has expertise in an area or facet of your job where you aren't particularly knowledgeable or effective. For example, I've had a long-standing coaching exchange with Dr. Ken Blanchard, CEO of The Ken Blanchard Companies, and author of the all-time business best seller, *The One Minute Manager*. Ken offers me terrific advice on writing and marketing business books in order to enhance my position as a business thought leader. As a cross-training benefit, I improve my technical knowledge, skills, and ability to communicate my ideas beyond delivering speeches and seminars. In turn, I serve as an accountability coach for Ken on his commitment to create a wellness lifestyle for himself, helping him overcome his excuses for not sticking to healthy habits for diet and exercise. Ken derives cross-training benefits by fine tuning his listening for team members' excuses about missed results, plus the improved energy and brain functioning that comes from a regular exercise program.

Key takeaway idea

Developing strengths is very different from correcting weaknesses. It's pretty straightforward to improve on a weakness simply by learning and practicing basic techniques. Doing more of what you already do well yields only incremental improvement. To produce appreciably better performance, you must acquire complementary skills in areas you have not yet mastered.

Deliberate Practice Method 4: Devising Safe Simulations to Perform Without Fear

Sports teams recognize stellar preparation is the predominant method to diminish fear and instill confidence. Coaches understand that repeated failure actually plays an integral part in continuous improvement. Athletes repeat drills over and over, knowing practice is a safe place to make mistakes and get corrective feedback. With repetitions, the rough edges of a performance get honed to perfection. Practice is designed to simulate fear-provoking situations that might arise in games. With supportive coaching, players learn to make the right spur-of-the-moment decisions and athletic moves. They can draw on their successes in practice to instill supreme confidence when a similar situation happens during a game. Simulation breeds familiarity, which lowers anxiety and builds confidence.

In the book, *The Art of the Game*, author Chris Ballard[9] describes the role transition required of Steve Kerr, a superb long-range shooter in the final season of a long NBA career. With his new team, the San Antonio Spurs, his playing time varied from 20 minutes one night, to six minutes the next game, depending on the competition. Kerr might fire up ten shots one game, or sit on the bench for several games. As a player accustomed to a consistent well-defined role, his shooting and self-confidence suffered from irregular playing opportunities.

Chip Engelland, the Spurs' shooting coach, recognized Kerr's changing role, and devised a specific simulation for practice. Picture Engelland and Kerr sitting in deep conversation on the bench at the Spurs' practice court. Suddenly, Engelland stands up, grabs a basketball, and yells to Kerr to run to the wing, a position on the basketball court on either side of the free throw line, and at a distance behind the three-point line. Engellard dribbles and passes Kerr the ball in perfect position to launch a three-point shot. After the pass-and-shoot interlude, the two men return to their conversation. After five minutes of small talk, Engellard repeats the drill.

This chitchat and shoot exercise was staggered to permit Kerr to get off only six shots in thirty minutes. After drilling for three days straight, Steve Kerr said, "Psychologically it was awesome, because then the next game I was like 'Hey, I just did this.'"

How fear runs rampant, but remains invisible

My experience from decades of executive coaching reveals how people hide their strong emotions at work, especially fear over not appearing competent. Victor, a seasoned CEO, wants his senior management team to offer input on the company's long-term strategy, yet he fears losing their respect, because he has always been a hard-driving direction-setter. He also dreads the risk inherent in letting other managers' ideas shape the company's future moves. Instead of eliciting strategic input, Victor undermines collaboration by devising his own strategic plan, consulting only minimally with his team. Meanwhile, the team rubber-stamps Victor's decisions.

Angela, an account executive, sticks to her sales presentation script in order to control the conversation, for fear customers will raise issues she's not prepared to address. She undermines her development as a sales professional by ignoring her manager's feedback to talk less and to ask more questions to invite customer reactions.

While I was coaching both Victor and Angela, neither of them showed obvious signs of fear, like excess sweating, trembling limbs, or an angry tone of voice. While they may feel fear, the obvious symptoms are not visible. Instead, fear shows up in their undermining behaviors like ignoring strategic input from peers, and sticking to a sales script to avoid a prospect's tough questions.

If these two common examples suggest that there's an awful lot of fear among your team members in going about their daily tasks, then you've gotten my point. Unfortunately, a fear-infested organization is a spawning ground for performance plateaus.

If you're going to be a deliberate practitioner, you need to get comfortable with deliberate practice since it always forces you and your team members out of comfort zones. Apprehension or uncertainty occurs even in contemplating a practice attempt at a higher-level performance. Your job is to design deliberate practice to diminish fear's performance-depleting interference.

Practice Drill: Recognizing Common Fear in Leadership Development

This practice drill will help you become proficient at identifying and mastering developmental challenges likely to provoke fear.

Acknowledge fear as a necessary element of development

It's a mistake to discount, diminish, or deny the presence of fear in the journey to become an elite leader. Take a lesson from sports teams who readily recognize common developmental challenges and are prepared to help players build confidence by engaging in simulations and safe practice regimens. Follow this two step practice drill:

1. Use the examples in the following chart to spot common fear-provoking developmental challenges faced by athletes and coaches which have comparable versions among your team members.

Figure 6.2 — Comparable Developmental Challenges in Sports and Business

Developmental Challenges in Sports	Developmental Challenges in Business
Advancing to a higher level of competition (from high school to college to professional)	Transitioning in stages of business (from entrepreneurial startup, to a professionally managed company, to a large national firm)
Adjusting to a new coaching style or system	Adjusting to a new leadership team or new boss
Competing as an underdog against a more-talented opponent with a better record	Competing for a key account against a competitor with more resources
Moving from player to coach, assistant to head coach, head coach to general manager	Transitioning to new responsibilities, such as from a front-line worker to a supervisor/boss
Playing under the pressure of media expectations	Staging a comeback after failing to meet investor expectations
Turning around a losing season	Turning around a poor-performing business
Coaching a team to become adept at winning on the road or in a hostile environment	Leading a team to deliver big results in an unfavorable economy for upscale products
Coaching super-talented players to choose to fit into a team concept	Coaching "stars" seeking promotions to collaborate in order to improve the team's results
Integrating new players into a veteran team	Onboarding new members to an intact team
Overcoming a referee's bad call at a key time	Overcoming the loss of a key account

2. For each item on your list of emerging developmental challenges, design a safe-to-fail experiment as discussed in Chapter 4. For instance, if a sales executive fears trying new selling approaches, have him experiment by making a presentation to a small account or to an ally in a large account, but who isn't the primary decision-maker. Another possibility would be to coach a micromanager who dreads delegation to delegate a minor decision to a team member.

Instill self-confidence by reviewing your prior developmental challenges

List developmental challenges you've mastered previously in your career, Acknowledge the range of fears you've overcome. For each item on your list, ask yourself:

- What practices did you adopt that helped you overcome your fear?
- What risks or extreme effort did you predict would occur, but never actually happened?

Treat your findings as compelling evidence of your capacity to feel fear, and still do what it takes to perform better.

Key takeaway idea

Development requires moving out of your comfort zone. If you're not feeling some sense of apprehension, you're not challenging yourself to the degree where surges in performance capacity become possible. Embrace fear as a signal you're gearing up for a breakthrough accomplishment. Gulp is good.

You've just overviewed deliberate practice habits of world-class athletic performers and teams. If you'd like to read a longer list (including Tiger Woods' full-day practice routine) go to my website: **www.turock.com.**

How do you regard the practice habits of athletes and sports teams? Do the words obsessive, over-the-top, or tedious come to mind? Or do you view the habits as a sign of dedication, attention to detail, or even creativity?

Where do you draw the line in defining practice standards that constitute "good enough?" It's a great question to ask repeatedly when you set aggressive goals, or find your progress to results sputtering.

For competent performers, good enough comes from their subjective judgment of what constitutes reasonable effort and risk. In other words, they're unlikely to participate in the business version of draining excess fat from the cottage cheese.

For elite performers, good enough is determined by their commitment to breakthrough results that defy historical norms. They realize doing more of the same practice protocol isn't going to catapult them to superior performance. Elite performers consider their extra effort to be worthy of their cherished ambitions.

Your History of Deliberate Practice Shapes Your Destiny as a Leader

"When my son asks me, 'Daddy, where are you going?' as I leave for work each morning, I tell him, 'I'm going to practice.'"
   – Ed Sanchez, Senior Director of In-store Environment, Home Depot

Deliberate practice is the most vital yet most neglected self-management skill. Most corporate training programs teach time management, stress management, and goal setting, yet hardly any courses are offered in deliberate practice. That's unfortunate because deliberate practice is the make-or-break skill for integrating formal classroom training with ongoing development during actual work. When you are meticulous in deliberate practice, you gain access to the following sources of power to catapult leadership development:

- *Your willingness to embrace fear increases.* You come to interpret fear as an emotion that accompanies any opportunity to pursue a breakthrough in performance.

- *Your performance plateaus get shorter.* You can conceive novel deliberate practice methods to transcend performance plateaus.

- *You expand your sense of healthy disregard for the unreasonable.* Each noticeable improvement in deliberate practice that's beyond your current comfort zone, expands your mindset regarding what constitutes reasonable effort and risk.

- *Your confidence in mastering plateaus increases.* When you succeed in transcending one plateau, you create a lasting reference to illustrate your ability to deliberately practice and to master future plateaus.

- *You develop a permanent antidote for complacency.* Deliberate practice is a non-stop mindset disturbance to the complacency that often accompanies success.

- *You reinvent yourself as a deliberate practitioner.* There's a remarkably subtle ripple effect of deliberate practice. People subconsciously realize it's the best way to get better at any facet of performance. Deliberate practitioners employ the four deliberate practice methods in both self-coaching and in helping others improve performance in business or in their personal life.

- *You offload much of leadership development to your direct reports to do for themselves.* When you teach deliberate practice methods to your direct reports, they are well-equipped with this single skill set to continually improve their capabilities. Most of your team members' development will occur when you're not even around. The two primary times you'll be needed are: 1) to provide creative input for arranging a new practice regimen to master a challenging plateau, or 2) to create a developmental assignment along with a deliberate practice plan to prepare a team member to eventually take on a new responsibility.

Miracle on the Hudson, or a deliberate practitioner at the controls?

What does it look like to be a deliberate practitioner who has access to these sources of power? There's no better illustration of someone who became an instant celebrity, due to a career spent in deliberate practice, than former U.S. Airways Captain "Sully" Sullenberger.

Regardless of rigorous training and hours of flying, how does an airline pilot deliberately practice flying a crippled jet? The media title of "Miracle on the

Hudson" may be awe-inspiring, but Captain Sullenberger's actions are no miracle; it was a matter of a well-practiced pilot being at the controls. To interpret the Hudson River landing as a miracle diminishes the pilot's eminent performance in his finest hour. Captain Sullenberger's cockpit brilliance demonstrates how decades of being a deliberate practitioner served as preparation for an emergency that called for his heroic improvisation.

First, consider the quantity of his practice time. Sullenberger was a U.S. Air Force F-4 fighter pilot from 1973 to 1980. He'd flown for U.S. Airways for 28 years with 19,000 hours of flying. His practice started in high school when he logged 2,000 hours in flying lessons.

Next consider the extraordinary feedback in his non-flight practice. Flight simulation training fulfills several elements of deliberate practice—mentally challenging the pilot, providing instant feedback, and employing methods designed by experts.

Sullenberger orchestrated unique cross-training practices most pilots don't even consider. Early in his career, he took up cross training as a glider pilot, which transferred into landing a jet without engine power. Being passionate about flight safety, he served as safety chairman for the Air Line Pilots Association, and wrote a paper with NASA scientists on "error inducing contexts in aviation." Plenty of airline catastrophes occur when pilots wait too long to switch into emergency mode to save passengers' lives. They make this judgment in the interest of avoiding a reprimand for not doing everything possible to keep from destroying a multimillion-dollar plane. At his defining moment as a pilot, Sullenberger knew his priorities, and instantly ditched the plane in the Hudson, rather than attempt to land on a runway. Finally, Sullenberger focused on mastering a high-impact fundamental skill—efficient flying measures. He had used every previous flight as an opportunity to practice conserving fuel, as well as giving passengers a smooth ride with minimal wind resistance and turbulence.

In his book, *Highest Duty*, Sullenberger says, "I flew thousands of flights in the last forty-two years, but my entire career is being judged by how I performed on one of them. This has been a reminder to me: We need to try to do the right thing every time, to perform at our best, because we never know what moment in our lives we'll be judged on."[10]

In business, we are not faced with life-and-death decisions that call for heroic action like Sullenberger was when a flock of birds instantly rendered his two jet engines useless. Nevertheless, business has its own moments that call for nothing short of elite performance.

Just as Captain Sullenberger never knew the fullest extent of his piloting capabilities until he and his crew were tested above the Hudson River, you won't know either. Leaders never know when their team will be called to utilize their full array of capabilities in meeting an against-all-odds situation.

Right now, return to the notion that practice makes permanent—for better or for worse. How you practice leadership today determines your effectiveness whenever you need to ask your team to respond to inevitable business challenges.

Duke Men's Basketball Coach, Mike Krzyzewski, says, "Whatever a leader does now sets up what he does later. And there's always a later."[11]

When extraordinary action is called for, you find out the exact extent of your influence. Do others have the necessary trust in you to follow your lead? Are your team members prepared with capabilities to respond to an extreme challenge? Will your teamwork align in flawless synchronicity? Will the group sustain their supreme effort, or quickly throw in the towel?

You'll never know the answer until "later" actually arrives, and your history of deliberate practice becomes apparent.

PHASE III:

ORCHESTRATE THE LEARNING-WHILE-WORKING PROCESS

Leadership Development Game Plan

Phase I:
Generate the Mindset of an Elite Performer

Leader's role:
Mindset Master

Phase II:
Practice Like a Pro

Leader's role:
Deliberate Practitioner

Phase III:
Orchestrate the Learning-While-Working Process

Leader's role:
Orchestrator of Elite Habits

CHAPTER 88

WHAT ATHLETES AND COACHES KNOW ABOUT TALENT DEVELOPMENT—THAT EXECUTIVES OFTEN OVERLOOK

As *deliberate practice* gets publicized in more and more business books, most executives appreciate its value, but stop short of using it in any widespread fashion in their companies. They believe deliberate practice works only in specific work conditions where schedules are fluid and time can be easily found for performance improvement. For instance, individual practitioners, such as musicians, chess players, or even solo entrepreneurs, have plenty of private time at their discretion. In addition, there are teams—like sports teams, military combat troops, and fire department brigades—that continually drill on basics, in order to perform flawlessly when beckoned by a challenging event. Otherwise, executives regard deliberate practice as highly impractical for a busy workplace. No one believes they have the luxury to reserve significant time for refining skills and expanding their repertoire of leadership capabilities.

Why do these executives automatically rule out deliberate practice as being impractical for the overwhelming majority of businesses? They don't yet grasp the unique role of a leader who orchestrates elite habits in the course of getting a day's work done.

In this chapter, you're going to be introduced to a facet of leadership—instilling elite habits—that many sports coaches take for granted, and executives often overlook. Deliberate practice works in any organization, regardless of size or industry type when two conditions are met:

1. When the work process is designed so learning and skill upgrading takes place quite naturally, while daily operations are getting done, and

2. When a team's designated leader doesn't need to be involved in every instance of coaching, training, or mentoring.

Picture yourself in a workplace that meets these two conditions. Everyone has taken on the role of a deliberate practitioner, and can practice to improve while they work alone. They can also be coaches to one another by providing feedback, debriefing a just-completed performance, or calling out victim language in the midst of a conversation. And those two conditions describe the essential design of the Learning-While-Working Process, the final part of the Leadership Development Game Plan.

The How Matters

In 2006, I was working with an ice cream manufacturer to develop the coaching skills of twenty-five sales operations managers. We were doing a self-assessment exercise, designed to disturb the mindset underlying this group's most pervasive performance plateau: planning for a sales call. I began by inviting the managers to assess their effectiveness on the task of pre-sales call planning by using a 10-point rating system. We posted large sheets with numbers 1–10 on a long wall around the room. I read descriptions for three performance standards represented by the number 1 for incompetent, 5 for competent, and 10 for elite performance. I asked them to take a few moments to assess their own performance, and then move to the appropriate spot by the number they'd chosen to rate themselves. I stepped back to watch.

Everyone in the room, including District Managers, Division Managers, and the Vice President of Sales Operations, started moving. Of the group, 70 percent clustered between points 2 through 4, signifying less-than-competent performance.

"What's the basis of your rating?" I asked the large group. Steve volunteered first. "I gave myself a 4. Most of my team is doing relationship selling, so they don't need to engage in much pre-sales call planning. I don't need to hammer on them to get better." When I asked Steve to explain why he has chosen to accept a 4 rating, he said, "As long as my sales people get customers to approve their display ideas and advertisements, I don't care how they get their results."

Steve's answer piqued my curiosity. "Show of hands, if you agree with that line of reasoning."

A couple of hands shot up instantly, and then slowly, one by one, the late voters registered. When 90 percent of the hands were up, I knew we had hit a nerve.

"So relationship selling is permissible if it gets results. Let me get this straight. You're saying that producing desired results gets a pass. How the results get produced doesn't matter."

I paused to let the point sink in before continuing. "Evidently I am the only one in the room to take exception to this compromise—since we're getting acceptable results, no improvement in the process is necessary." Only months earlier, the group had undergone training in a more sophisticated style of strategic selling that they had essentially abandoned. "I'm not going to let you continue to unconsciously follow that line of reasoning. How your people get results does matter. The *how* matters."

I stuck my neck out, intentionally taking on a leadership role as a mindset master. If I took responsibility for dismantling an artificial constraint on a team's performance capacity, maybe the leaders in the room would do so, too.

The entire group realized a piece of their dirty laundry was now up for inspection. Tension was palpable, and I could feel discomfort in the room. A fervent hope for swift resolution was colliding with a how's-this-going-to-turn-out uncertainty over the public unraveling of a topic previously not discussed. "Who's responsible for tolerating this less-than-competent performance?" I asked.

Larry stepped up. "When my team members acknowledge they are not using the strategic selling skills we've been trained to use, I sympathize by helping them come up with justifications for their failure."

"Larry, what's the payoff you derive, at least in the short-term, by accepting their reluctance to try out newly-trained skills?"

Larry answered openly. "I get to be seen as a nice boss to work for, one who's not overbearing or pushy." Courageously, Larry took accountability.

"Who's next?" I asked. Many in the group admitted their rationalizations, their shortcomings in following up the higher standards for pre-call planning. I pushed a little more. "Sounds like each of you are abdicating your accountability for the professional development of your sales team." Finally, we were talking about the elephant in the room. No one could deny the unsettling truth any longer.

Three years after this coaching conversation, the ice cream company's up-leveled performance standards for pre-call planning have become modus operandi. The phrase, "The how matters," has become a mantra.

Focus on the Process and the Score Takes Care of Itself

Until I began studying sports as a performance field, I didn't fully realize the degree to which "The how matters" is vital to achieving sustainable success in business, where "making the numbers" is a preoccupation. The all-time legendary coaches in sports base their sustainable success formula on their ability to implement an elite-player development process—"the how" of preparation for and performing during game conditions.

Phil Jackson, Head Coach of two NBA dynasties, the Chicago Bulls and the Los Angeles Lakers, and winner of eleven championship rings, essentially says to forget the ring. "Obsessing about winning is a loser's game. The most we can hope for is to create the best possible conditions for success, then let go of the outcome." If not on winning, where do you focus your attention? According to Jackson, "What matters most is playing the game the right way and having the courage to grow, as human beings as well as basketball players. When you do that, the ring takes care of itself."[1]

Alabama Head Football Coach Nick Saban, whose teams, including Louisiana State University, have won four college national championships, calls his winning formula, "The Process." Saban says, "The scoreboard has nothing to do with the process," which includes:

- Specialist coaches from outside of pure football backgrounds (mental toughness coaches, strength and conditioning coaches, media consultants) broaden players' capabilities.

- Statistical analysts research potential recruits, break down tapes of opponent's games, and chart every repetition of every practice drill.

- Players undergo a psychological profile to reveal how to motivate their top performance.

- Video conferencing is conducted with recruits during the NCAA's no-visitation periods.

- Clear job descriptions are required for coaches and staff.

- An 18-month master-planning calendar enables the staff to align on priorities and collaborate on execution.

- Weekly academic reviews enable academic advisors to brief the coaching staff on players at risk for getting poor grades.

- Improvisational speech training exercises enable players who are team leaders, to inject a more energetic and theatrical presence to their communications with teammates. Every Thursday is Speech Day.

- Five unwavering values (discipline, effort, commitment, toughness, pride) serve as the organizing principles for making choices and taking action.

- Daily offseason workout reports document the amount of weight lifted on specific exercises, as well as periodic body fat testing.

- Vision training equipment to improve players' reaction time will be included in a new, state-of-the-art 37,000-square-foot strength and conditioning facility.[2]

Putting process before results may work brilliantly in sports, but it sounds counterintuitive, if not ridiculous, for a business. In a business leader's priorities, the only score that really matters is making sure the key performance indicators meet or exceed expectations, quarter after quarter. Playing to win on the scoreboard may work if the game is only about producing short-term results. But sustainable success is impossible when a large percentage of senior executives aren't the kind of leaders—orchestrators of elite habits—who facilitate a work process to raise their team's performance capacity.

Introducing Your New Role—Orchestrator of Elite Habits

As a football player for Jericho High School on Long Island in the late 1960s, I sadly recognized that as a 145-pound cornerback, I was not going to make the cut with a major college football team. The opportunity to live out my dream of playing for a legendary football program came true when I participated in a series of fantasy camps conducted by the University of Southern California Trojans football coaching staff. The objective of the camps was to provide participants, primarily between the ages of 25-45, with an authentic experience of being a Trojan football player preparing for a game day challenge.

I was impressed by USC's player development process, which produced extraordinary results. From 2002 to 2008, Head Coach Pete Carroll's teams won a record seven consecutive conference titles, and recorded at least eleven victories in each of those seven seasons. During Carroll's nine-year coaching tenure, his teams won 83 percent of their games, including two national championships. His coaching staff developed thirty-four All-American first teamers, and fifty-three NFL draft picks. Three assistant coaches became college or professional head coaches. Four years after leaving USC, Carroll's same player development process produced a Super Bowl championship for the Seattle Seahawks in 2014.

Pete Carroll captures his coaching philosophy in two words: Win Forever. Coach Carroll is not referring to a flawless record, but to performing at a level where his team contends for championships year after year, without any prolonged periods for rebuilding. Taking a more microscopic perspective, "Win Forever" means living each moment engaged in this question: How would I be thinking or acting if I were playing to win forever?

Coach Carroll says, "If I was writing down the keys to our success, I would write one point: We're going to do things better than they have ever been done before. We are going to teach, practice, recruit, counsel, analyze, and do everything better than it has ever been done before."

I saw a clear connection between Coach Carroll's Win Forever philosophy and the elite performance research on deliberate practice. Although I considered sharing this approach with business leaders, I initially dismissed any chance to make a relevant translation. I relegated Coach Carroll's outrageous "best-it's-ever-been-done" standard as the ranting of a baby-boomer coach, who never met a positive-thinking course he didn't like. College jocks who aspire to NFL careers will drink the Kool-Aid, but business executives never will.

My misgivings vanished when Coach Carroll articulated his unique vision for a coach's role in the player development process. He has reinvented the role, as well as the methods for the next generation of football coaches, replacing the clichéd, scream-in-your-face dictator. He expressed this new role with one provocative question:

> *"What if my job as a coach isn't so much to force or coerce performance as it is to create situations where players develop the confidence to set their talents free and pursue their potential to its full extent?"*[3]

Carroll's solution is a player development process, which requires a coach/ leader to be what I have called an orchestrator of elite habits. In this role, leaders stop relying on role-derived authority or charismatic personality to drive result-oriented action. They exert influence by imbedding habit-triggering mechanisms, which help team members perform brilliantly when there's no leader present.

Coach Carroll refers to a quote from Aristotle, "We are what we repeatedly do. Excellence, then, is not an act, but a habit." Habits are repetitive, automatic routines of behavior, and are hard to give up. So habits occur without conscious effort–for better or for worse, for excellence, or for a watered-down adequate performance.

The Win Forever philosophy incorporates a regimented player development process to produce habitual ways of thinking and acting, in order to achieve excellent performance with minimal effort. This point doesn't suggest that players stop making the supreme physical effort required in the game of football. It means that giving full effort becomes a habit. There is no it's-only-practice degree of effort.

The whole notion of "effortless excellence" means players fully engage in a process for cultivating peak performance, without requiring extra effort to figure out the best things to do to get better, or to summon sufficient motivation to do them. Excellent habits occur effortlessly.

As Coach Carroll says, "We prepare at the highest level, so we can practice at the highest level, so we can play at the highest level." His player development process, known as "Prepare/Practice/Play," produces a rhythm of habitual routines for thinking and acting. Here's his 3P process in a nutshell:

- "Prepare" gives players the fundamentals of nutrition, physical conditioning, movement, and mental toughness as a prerequisite to participate in a high-intensity practice.

- "Practice" is the opportunity players use to flawlessly execute their assignments under game-like conditions. They do so with the up-tempo pace and competitive zeal of game day. Hypercompetitive practice constitutes a weekly audition to earn playing time in games.

- "Play" means activating the same focus and effort expended in practice during the actual game, so players do not need to summon up a never-before-seen performance capacity in real competition. Instead they trust their teammates, focus fully on their assignments, and exude confidence in their own capabilities.

Do you see the organizing principle for this rhythm? It's about competing constantly to meet lofty standards and master the prerequisites for taking on greater responsibility. Players compete to surpass their own personal best performance, and also compete with teammates to take on bigger roles in practice and in games. Coaches compete with other teams' coaching staffs to keep improving the quality of preparing, practicing, and playing, to meet best-it's-ever-been-done standards.

Orchestrating Rhythm in a Talent-Development Process

The coach's whistle blows. Then the yell, "Huddle up! On the run! Nobody walks!" From the sidelines, I watch several hundred high school players jog to midfield and take a knee surrounding Coach Carroll. "Today, you are a Trojan," he says to start the clinic. "Our goal is to produce the best practice in any sport and at any level: high school, college, or pro, in terms of intensity, learning, conditioning, and fun."

In football, practice plays a vital role in effortlessly instilling excellent habits. Any enduring habit consists of a triggering event, which activates a routine, which ultimately leads to a reward. So the formula is simply:

Trigger → Routine→ Reward

In USC football, one primary trigger is the day of the week, since each day calls for a specific practice routine. The practice routines are designed to create the proper rhythm—varying the intensity of physical and mental effort, so players' performance readiness peaks on game days.

"Tell-the-Truth Monday" calls for players and coaches to assess their performance, and take accountability for mistakes and successes in game plan execution. It includes rigorous study of game film, and assigning grades for individual players, as well as the offensive, defensive, and special teams units.

"Competition Tuesday" has nothing to do with the upcoming opponent. It is focused on re-energizing players' competitive instincts to bring full engagement to the drills and scrimmaging. The coaching staff fervently believes, "Competition is a learned habit." Consequently, the defensive team gives a peak effort, which serves to push their offensive team counterparts to maximum performance. Practice is orchestrated with such intensity that competing in a game against a lesser opponent is often easier than going up against USC teammates. The practice field's appearance simulates game conditions by involving referees, pumping in crowd noise, displaying points on the scoreboard, and calling mock TV timeouts.

"Turnover Wednesday" casts attention on one single facet of the game day performance that contributes prominently to winning or losing: ball control. The offensive team practices techniques to prevent mistakes like fumbles and interceptions that put the football in the opponent's possession. The defensive team's coaches devise practice drills and game strategies to cause opponents to turn the football over to USC.

"No-Repeat Thursday" focuses on flawless execution of the game plan. The starting team performs scripted plays against a scout team that is mimicking the opposition's counter-formations. Flawless execution is the biggest factor players have control over to counter game day adversity, such as the competitive spirit of fired-up opponents, hostile crowds, and unfavorable calls by referees.

"Walk-Through Friday" drastically slows down the physical effort so players can rest and conserve energy for the next day's game. The day's activities are tightly choreographed to get players mentally prepared to expend great effort. Players and coaches conduct every activity as a ritual, from the bus ride to the stadium, walking through plays in slow motion, reviewing assignments, pre-game meals, even extending to evening prayer.

The day-to-day sequence of activities ensures all facets of preparation get covered in the best sequence to nurture game day readiness. Each week takes on a rhythm of routines so learning a game plan and improving skills happen with no wasted effort. Players and coaches concentrate on each task, knowing it's the best use of their time.

Small wins are the final link in a rhythmic habit-change progression. USC's player development process is designed to capture and publicize small wins. Every year, the Trojans' over-riding goal is to win a national championship. Since being the No. 1 team in the country is a rare accomplishment, the small wins get broken down into categories like:

- *Noticing progress indicators in each task.* Each team activity takes on heightened importance. Each impeccable repetition of an agility drill reflects increased ability to perform with the precision of muscle memory. Each film study session is an opportunity for players and coaches to reveal areas for improvement in mechanics and on-the-field judgment.

- *Living team values.* The Win Forever philosophy is value-driven with a central theme—Always Compete—and unwavering beliefs, such as: no whining, no complaining, no excuses.

- *Achieving statistical measures that contribute to winning games.* USC's coaching staff devises elaborate metrics for individual players and the offensive, defensive, and special teams units, in order to measure their effectiveness in practice and in games.

Injecting rhythm in the workplace: Triggers + small wins

Now that you understand USC's rhythm or triggers, routines, and small wins, it's time to translate this format to your workplace. Habits are constantly being formed—mindlessly, or by design. How will you, as an orchestrator of elite habits, re-design your work process so it automatically elicits choices to increase leadership capabilities? The first step in establishing a coherent rhythm is identifying the triggers to launch job-imbedded development routines.

Three categories of triggers

Evocative names are a subtle trigger with surprising impact. When we attach an evocative name to a specific conversation or meeting, the participants are more likely to engage with the proper emotional tone and effort to turn a mundane transaction into a special quality of experience.

Which meeting would motivate you more fully—the Morning Update, or a Grounding for Greatness? All too often, the loosely-structured daily update is nothing more than attendees touching base with information that could have been communicated through e-mail. In contrast, a Grounding for Greatness meeting is designed as an occasion to practice vital skills like listening, giving feedback, coaching, and setting goals for deliberate practice.

During Jack Welch's twenty-year tenure as GE's CEO, participants in a Welch-run operations review referred to it as a "no-spin zone". Rather than trying to save face in front of the boss, and probably being called out for evading accountability, everyone prepared an astute analysis of the root causes of unwanted outcomes, and also their plans for course correction.

Time is the second category of triggers. Creating a calendar to serve as a triggering event is a wonderful way to ensure that vital, but not urgent, items get done with the proper frequency.

In consulting with Hormel Foods Consumer Products Sales, I found they wanted to help the senior sales executives conceive and implement elite standards for preparing for sales meetings with their key retail accounts. To ensure adherence to a very challenging new set of standards, the Hormel team adopted a rhythmic progression around three themes: idea generation → condensing content → fine-tuning performance quality.

Three months before the key account meeting, the Hormel team focused on generating ideas from studying far-reaching strategic issues. They investigated emerging consumer trends, identified retailer vulnerabilities, and brainstormed novel solutions that utilize Hormel's organizational capabilities. Two months out, the group decided on the most relevant content, and what provocative questions to ask customers. They narrowed a long list of ideas down to the most pertinent topics to cover in the limited meeting time. In the final month, their top priority was proficient execution. Everyone's attention turned to shape the flow of the meeting, to tweak the PowerPoint presentation, and to role-play challenges likely to be raised by customers.

About two weeks in advance of the meeting, customers were sent pre-work so they could derive the most value from the upcoming strategic conversation. The actual meeting was hardly a typical sales pitch. It resembled a consulting session. Hormel's elite standard called for top customers to gain such valuable strategic insights that they would have been willing to pay a consulting fee. The Hormel team went beyond elite preparation to include debriefing. No team member booked a plane flight home from a key account meeting until the next day, in order to allow sufficient time to conduct a first-class debriefing session. As a huge win, Hormel was honored by Wal-Mart as Supplier of the Year in 2011 and 2012.

Sounds are a third type of trigger that not only evoke specific behaviors but elicit intentions that effect the quality of performance. Carrying the right intention into a conversation makes a huge difference in the first impression you make on other people. To trigger a welcoming tone in my voice when I answer my cell phone, my ring tone is a college fight song—*Fight on for USC*, of course.

Sounds can trigger bad habits as well. For example, when your computer announces an incoming e-mail, does it instantly divert your attention from a challenging task? If this distraction is too alluring in the midst of performing a vital task, turn it off. Even better, set an hourly alert sound to signal you to pause and notice if you're attending to a vital priority, or wasting time pursuing stress-relieving distractions.

Small wins

What role do small wins play in a business setting? In a *Harvard Business Review* blog post, Teresa Amabile and Steve Kramer wrote: "Our recent research discovered how critical it is for teams and individuals working on complex problems to achieve small wins regularly. Because setbacks are so common in truly important problems, people become disheartened unless they can point to some meaningful advance most days, even if that advance is seemingly minor, and even if it involves nothing more than extracting insights from the day's failures."[4]

To sharpen your ability to create and recognize small wins, explore these questions:

- What does being a walking model of your organization's values look like?
- How can you assess learning or skill improvements during a typical business day?
- What short-term statistics, linked with achieving long-term results, can you track?
- What lessons have been learned from failures?
- What self-limiting beliefs did you discard through your extraordinary effort?

Case example: The rhythm of Garbage University

Gazelles Inc. provides executive education, coaching, and technology services to help mid-market companies around the world build and execute a strategic plan to grow revenues, profits, valuation, and knowledge. In his book, *Mastering the Rockefeller Habits*, Gazelles' Chief Growth Officer, Verne Harnish, calls for fast-growth companies to institute a rhythm of specific meetings and key performance indicators (KPI) to drive accountability for both short-term and long-term tactical and strategic issues.[5] Each day, the team takes a brisk five- to fifteen-minute standup gathering to share relevant news, and works to remove roadblocks to results. In a one-hour weekly meeting, the group does standard updating, and then devotes half the time to forward progress on a single high-priority issue for the month or quarter. In a two- to four-hour monthly meeting, upper and middle managers use structured time to collaborate on projects, with an hour or two devoted to specific training. Finally, in one- or two-day quarterly meetings, the senior managers concentrate on strategic priorities to assess current progress and anticipate future trends.

One of the Gazelles' members, The City Bin Co., a waste management company based in Ireland, establishes a specific rhythm of ongoing leadership development. Founder and CEO Gene Browne is the prime facilitator of weekly three-hour learning sessions, comprising an initiative the nine participating managers call Garbage University.[6] Most sessions require the participants to prepare by reading leadership books or articles. The materials are chosen and designed to prompt practical outcomes to create change, either in the management team's thinking or in the way they actually approach their work process. Browne and his team see the Learning Sessions as a strategic tool to assist in learning about leadership, and to initiate and support organizational changes. The varied curriculum includes topics like teamwork, strategic planning, improving writing skills, and food as a source of energy. In most meetings, the new knowledge gets converted into producing management tools. For example, while studying interviewing, team members developed hiring scorecards for their functional areas. In their study of social media, they devised an 18-month social media plan. When components of strategic planning were covered, the members created future scenarios for various markets, customer profiles, and business-model templates.

Are you wondering how Gene Browne can afford to spend 20 percent of his time developing leaders, and also require his key managers to allocate a similar amount? If you asked Browne, he'd answer with a version of "How can I afford *not* to develop leaders?" In fact, here's what he told me about the overriding benefit behind Garbage University:

> As an entrepreneur, I feel that I have an obligation to the people who help me realize my business dreams. Due to the nature of entrepreneurial activity, I can't promise lifetime employment, but I can promise that by being part of my leadership team, a person will always be employable. Great people are in demand, and having the best people on my team also influences other areas of the business. The culture has to be right, the rewards have to be right, etc. So investing so much in creating great leaders is our fulcrum for having a great business.

Browne and company are developing a great business. The rhythm of the Learning Sessions began in May 2011. Despite a terrible economy in Ireland, The City Bin Co. doubled in size, and has been a four-time winner of the Deloitte Best Managed Companies Award (Ireland) 2009–2012. In 2012, The City Bin Co. became the first European investment target of the Averda Group, the largest environmental services company across the Middle East and Africa. Averda's rationale for the investment? The two primary factors were the quality of management and intellectual property.

Practice Drill: Taking Stock of Your Current Leadership Development Habits

Before you embark on orchestrating elite habits, it's extremely helpful to assess your organization's existing habits. Get several colleagues to rate the following mini-audit to discover gaps between your current leadership development process and elite standards.

Figure 7.1 — Mini-Audit for Quality of a Leadership Development Process

On a 1-5 scale, to what degree do these descriptions approximate, What Goes On In Your Business? 1 = Never Happens 0% of the Time 3 = True 50% of the Time 5 = The Way It is 90% of the Time	
1. Our managers are comfortable in monitoring activities so plans get done. They are uneasy and less skilled in training, coaching, and developing their team members' capabilities.	Rating =
2. When executives display obvious interpersonal/leadership flaws (e.g., dominating conversations, being condescending toward colleague's ideas) or skill deficits (e.g., giving boring presentations), no one offers corrective feedback or shares the impact on the team's effectiveness.	Rating =
3. Our meetings are spent giving updates on recent activities and reviewing key metrics. We don't include an agenda item that affords opportunity to deliberately practice specific thinking or communication skills, and share feedback.	Rating =
4. When we conduct leadership training or bring in outside speakers, we don't create systematic follow-up plans for implementing actionable ideas or new skills back at work. Participants leave knowing they have a pass to do *whatever they can find time to do OR feel comfortable doing.*	Rating =
5. We have micromanagers who know how to delegate, but they perform tasks and make decisions their subordinates should be responsible for accomplishing.	Rating =
6. What we call "debriefing" a meeting is actually summarizing action items for implementation. We don't take time to assess the effectiveness of our meetings, and the quality of our individual performance. Casual "how do you think that went?" conversations pass for debriefing.	Rating =

Now look back over your answers. Did any single item register as eye-opening news? Which of the shortcomings is your team aware of, but hasn't made a concerted effort to remedy? If you received value from this short version, a downloadable 25-item questionnaire, "Conditions for Leadership Development Audit," is available at my website, **www.turock.com**.

Key Takeaway Idea

Mark Cuban, Owner/Head Honcho of the Dallas Mavericks, comes up with audacious entrepreneurial ideas, by leveraging this principle: "Creating opportunities means looking where others are not."[7] Most business leaders are not looking to conceive a transformational work process to develop the habits of elite leaders. Seizing the opportunity to build excellent leadership development habits will expand your competitive advantage.

USC's Player Development Process—The Model for the Learning-While-Working Process

USC's player development process is the prototype for my Learning-While-Working Process. Pete Carroll's provocative question about a coach's role is the key to your becoming *an orchestrator of elite habits*. Here's the revised version for you to contemplate:

> *What if my job as a leader isn't so much to force*
> *or coerce performance as it is to create situations*
> *where other leaders on my team(s) develop the*
> *confidence to set their talents free, and pursue*
> *their potential to its full extent?*

To become an orchestrator of elite habits, you lead by example, replacing your own bad habits with more effective ones. The first habit to discard involves misdiagnosing performance management issues, attributing them to a team member's lack of talent or motivation. Most often, your fellow managers want to perform better, but are stymied by a flawed work process that favors efficiency over leadership development. As an orchestrator of elite habits, you are accountable for reprogramming the triggers, routines, and small wins so your team members effortlessly make the right choices to grow as leaders.

The Learning-While-Working Process is the rhythm for enabling managers to improve their leadership capabilities while real work gets done. Instead of your leadership development process getting suffocated by unrelenting work demands, it becomes effortless—ingrained as a habit to replace autopilot efficiency measures like multitasking, winging it, and micromanaging.

In Chapter 8, we will explore the intricacies of the Learning-While-Working Process, using real-life examples from my executive coaching and Mission Unreasonable Projects.

CHAPTER 08

BUILDING CAPABILITIES WHILE REAL WORK GETS DONE

Secret Sauce

None of my clients have ever asked me, "Art, can you help us design a work process that helps our team members build their capabilities in the midst of getting daily tasks done?" I haven't had a single request—not one. Apparently, reinventing the work process isn't an obvious source for performance improvement, even when senior managers notice their team members aren't preparing to assume greater leadership responsibility.

My customers' solutions involve increasing random acts of training and development. Send people to training. Have their boss provide coaching or mentoring sessions. Offer periodic developmental assignments. Conduct performance reviews more than once a year. Basically, do more of the same conventional approach. Unfortunately, there's no time to do these activities with greater frequency if current workloads are to get done. So they settle for a staff of substantially competent managers and very few great ones.

Most leaders never want to feel or appear incompetent, so they rarely attempt to solve this leadership development compromise. Accordingly, courageous business leaders who are willing to reinvent their work process to cultivate an high-performance leadership team will achieve a game-changer advantage. And that's why the Learning-While-Working Process deserves to be regarded as the secret sauce of the Leadership Development Game Plan.

The Learning-While-Working Process emanates from a leadership team's belief that abundant learning opportunities occur in the emerging circumstances of every workday. Since these occasions are so readily available, leaders can orchestrate a rhythm of triggering events and job-imbedded development routines to free up their team's capacity for reaching higher levels of performance. Ultimately, the Learning-While-Working Process becomes a series of effortless habits to produce a continually renewing stream of elite leaders.

Orchestrating the Learning-While-Working Process doesn't require revamping an organizational culture. That's because most cultures don't espouse anti-learning values. Most corporate cultures possess values that would steer managers toward developing people to their fullest potential. The problem comes in actually "walking the talk." The Learning-While-Working Process makes it possible for people to align their actions with existing cultural values in support of continual learning. Culture change is unnecessary when habit change is sufficient to generate ample time for leadership development.

In this chapter, we'll explore the Learning-While-Working Process, and the leader's role in orchestrating a rhythm of job-imbedded routines rarely seen in companies. We'll first overview the rhythm between each of the 5 key triggers and their correlated job-imbedded development routines, plus the small wins that advance leadership development. Later, we will look at case examples to illustrate the most unique job-imbedded development routines, and also offer practice drills you can use to become an orchestrator of elite habits.

Ingredients of the Secret Sauce—the 5Ps

You will recall, in Chapter 7 we talked about how a football team's practice is designed to effortlessly instill excellent habits. To replace a less desirable habit with a new, more effective one requires consistent recognition of a triggering event, which activates a routine that ultimately leads to a reward. We looked at this simple formula:

Trigger → Routine → Reward

The rhythm to drive the Learning-While-Working Process comes from a sequence of triggering events I call the 5Ps. There are two primary rhythms. First, each of the 5Ps is a trigger to cause people to choose from among a number of time-efficient, job-imbedded development routines (abbreviated as "JIDR"). In addition, the 5Ps act as triggers for each other, since they're designed to flow in sequence from P1 to P5. Throughout the process, everyone derives small wins from the learning and development taking place during the accumulating hours of deliberate practice.

Let's start with a quick overview of the 5Ps, emphasizing the unique benefits that come from building an elite leadership team:

P1/Prepare by mastering fundamentals: *Move from presuming that basic leadership skills are already sufficiently mastered, to requiring ongoing refinement of basics.*

Prepare is the trigger for activating managers to continually refine basic leadership skills. It activates two kinds of rhythms: macro and micro.

On a macro scale, the senior management team's ongoing focus is on mastering basic knowledge and skills of leadership. They compose a list of prerequisites to describe elite performance in a leadership role. Each quarter, the management team picks one specific skill set to improve. The entire group may read a classic book on the skill to be refined, accompanied by an assessment tool for determining their individual strengths and weaknesses. In turn, staff meetings are designed as skill-building sessions, where at least one agenda item affords the team opportunities to practice the skill or process that's getting refined. Through all of this reading, assessing, and practicing, performance standards get specified or spelled out for the first time. Each ensuing quarter, the management team concentrates on improving a different leadership basic by following the same rhythmic sequence. Over time, continually refining basics becomes ingrained as the new normal.

On a micro level, each day starts with a Grounding for Greatness, a ritual which enables senior managers to convey the unrelenting focus on basics to their direct reports. The first step is to change the daily cadence of activity, which currently involves rushing from the parking lot to tackle the day's to-do list. Instead, a manager who's mastered the skills for being a deliberate practitioner kicks off a brief morning meeting, to help participants formulate their learning goals for the day, design deliberate prace opportunities that stretch their comfort zone, and reinforce their commitment to continuous improvement.

P2/Practice while real work gets done: Move from getting tasks done expediently, to consciously designing and improvising deliberate practice drills in the midst of daily tasks. Two types of deliberate practice, instant practice protocol and Re-Do occur spontaneously when team members intentionally engage with every task to create an occasion for building skills:

If you work alone much of the day, how do you get feedback to improve? You deliberately practice to the best of your ability, while at the same time you observe yourself while doing it, making mental notes before engaging in critiquing your overall performance. You might do this instant practice protocol in the midst of a one-on-one coaching session, a phone call with a customer, or when you are alone planning priorities and there is no feedback available from your boss, customers, or co-workers.

How many times in your life have you wished you could have called for a do-over? Here's your chance. *Re-Do* is a powerful practice opportunity. You and your team will decide ahead of time to use Re-Do as an intentional way to trigger immediate changes in your bad habits (like angry outbursts when team members report lousy results), or ineffective behaviors (like being sparing rather than generous in acknowledging a team's accomplishments). Instead of waiting months to bring up weaknesses during an annual performance review, team members call out their colleagues to instantly practice a prescribed corrective response to replace a bad habit. One reason Re-Do is such a powerful mechanism for behavior change is because it is a public acknowledgment that everyone can do better, and the team will no longer tolerate practicing bad habits.

> *Re-Do turns mistakes and weaknesses into*
> *instant skill practice. It eliminates blame and*
> *shame over mistakes, activates the power of*
> *practice, and propels you and your team to fail*
> *your way to success.*

P3/Perform in game-on situations: Move from simply going through the motions in getting a task done, to bringing second-nature proficiency to high-stakes situations—improving business results and enhancing learning outcomes.

Remember Pete Carroll's Win Forever philosophy. During intense practices, players must perform basics with second-nature skill proficiency to earn playing time in games. In your business, similar game-on situations frequently go unacknowledged. There are two kinds of situations to be aware of: 1) *high-stakes situations which impact business results,* and 2) *high-stakes situations for accelerating leadership development.*

High-stakes situations for business results require a leader to pick team members who possess second-nature skill proficiency to qualify for a significant assignment. Think of a sales call to a major customer where the goal is to prompt buyers to recognize needs they were unaware of, and which they might find unsettling to address. Another example is an all-hands meeting, where C-level executives must communicate a compelling rationale to elicit support for a challenging change initiative. In such high-stakes situations, leaders determine who plays, and who is on the bench. Only proven elite performers get to perform in game-on situations.

High-stakes situations for accelerating leadership development need to be designated as "game-on," or else they're easily squandered. I'm referring to mundane events like the daily check-in with team members at their workstations, or when they return to work after attending a class. We don't automatically treat such pedestrian events as deserving game-on status. To leverage these learning opportunities, team members should strive to gain second-nature proficiency in skills used every day, like setting performance improvement goals, coaching, taking accountability, listening, and giving and receiving feedback. Just as in sports, the entire team needs to regard robust deliberate practice opportunities as game-on situations, which prepare them to eventually perform in the high-stakes situations driving business results.

P4/Perfect the process: Move from expediently completing an activity, to scrutinizing the just-completed process, in order to extract every bit of learning possible.

How do most of your meetings end? Do you just stop the conversation when the allotted meeting time runs out, or when you've finished the agenda? Or is the signal to wind down when the group produces an action summary of to-do activities and by-when deadlines? If these finishing rituals sound familiar, you and your team members are neglecting a valuable source of learning. You'll benefit by installing a new trigger, P/4 Perfect, to occur when your meetings draw to a close.

P4/Perfect is a trigger that activates a debriefing protocol to assess the strengths and weaknesses in a just-completed activity, and offer suggestions for improving performance. A well-conceived debriefing enables meeting participants to go beyond reviewing prior learning points to actually generating fresh insights. The trigger P4/Perfect ensures no meeting—such as a sales call, one-on-one coaching, or project review—is complete without a formal debriefing and a P5 publicizing to complete the Learning-While-Working Process.

P5/Publicize fresh learning: Move from absorbing learning for your own consumption, to sharing learning generously with a widespread community of contacts.

When was the last time you left a meeting and paused to think, "Who else might benefit from what we just learned?" When asked this question, most of my clients realize how rare it's become to share learning with colleagues about their own development as leaders.

P5/Publicize invokes a constant reminder to share learning generously with other parties who stand to benefit, within as well as outside your organization. Besides your immediate team members, you might share lessons learned with colleagues in cross-functional teams, customers, suppliers, trade association members, or social media communities. Once publicizing becomes a habit for a core group, it rapidly expands the number of "teachers" within a company.

Get caught up in the rhythm of the 5Ps

The following chart, Overview of the Learning-While-Working Process, succinctly describes the essence of each trigger, the best principle that promotes action, and the correlated job-imbedded development routines (JIDR).

Figure 8.1 — Overview of the Learning-While-Working Process

P1/PREPARE

Principle: Periodically practice basics or foundational skills of your role or profession	**JIDR:** Quarterly study of leadership basics Grounding for Greatness Meetings designed for skill practice

P2/PRACTICE

Principle: Stage deliberate practice in the midst of real work	**JIDR:** Re-Do bad habits Instant practice protocal

P3/PERFORM

Principle: Declare game-on situations when there's high impact on business results or learning outcomes	**JIDR:** Specify vital work processes Transfer of training

P4/PERFECT

Principle: Debrief to improve just-completed processes	**JIDR:** Debriefing protocols Assumption collecting

P5/PUBLICIZE

Principle: After a learning experience, ask, "Who else could benefit?"	**JIDR:** Distiller's report Online sharing vehicles

Besides triggering job-imbedded development routines, each P serves as a cue for the next one following in the sequence. Once a leadership team *prepares* (P1) a list of basic skills, they orchestrate *practice* opportunities in their day's work (P2). When *performing* in game-on conditions (P3), leaders adhere to the prerequisite of employing second-nature skill proficiency to the vital task at hand. After every practice session (P2 or P3) finishes, participants instantly move into a structured debriefing (P4) to consolidate learning that just took place. Finally, a completed debriefing protocol (P4) triggers a reflexive question, "Who else might benefit from what we just learned?" and participants proceed to share the lessons they learned (P5).

The rhythm of the Learning-While-Working process endures because the micro-investment of time spent engaged in job-imbedded development routines delivers small wins. We experience joy in delivering higher level/elite performance in a game-on situation. We exude pride in mastering a long-standing plateau. We feel a strong measure of team synergy when a lesson shared with a colleague helps them to succeed in a way that, otherwise, never would have happened. When people keep performing better, they reap rich rewards, such as taking on informal leadership duties, being assigned to service a key account, being nominated to an emerging talent group, and eventually assuming a position carrying greater responsibility. Finally, small wins can be defined in key performance statistics used to measure learning goals. We can count the hours of deliberate practice per month, the number of feedback exchanges with direct reports in a given week, or the percentage of undistracted time devoted to high-priority activities per day.

Like any habit change, the startup phase of the Learning-While-Working Process will seem unnatural, and will require upfront time to master. However, the learning curve will be brief because you're already executing the other roles called for in the Leadership Development Game Plan: mindset master and deliberate practitioner. As a mindset master, you know how to activate mindset shifts conducive to leadership development. As a deliberate practitioner, you are alert to the four methods of deliberate practice to transcend plateaus, and keep improving your leadership capabilities.

All that's left is for you to become an orchestrator of elite habits. You will employ the Learning-While-Working Process to trigger mechanisms for habit change. The 5Ps trigger instantaneous routines to happen effortlessly, without requiring self-discipline or willpower. When the 5Ps are in full operation, the premise "All there is at work, is time to get better" becomes reality. It's time to make them your secret sauce for leadership development.

Orchestrating Job-Imbedded Development Routines into Your Busy Work Day

You and your colleagues are already engaged in developmental activities including coaching, mentoring, job shadowing, and performance monitoring. But there's a formidable problem. Most conventional developmental activities aren't automatic routines, except on-the-job training for new employees, and the annual performance appraisal required for all employees. The remaining developmental activities get done on the basis of "if time becomes available." They are not deeply ingrained job-imbedded development routines which occur effortlessly.

The job-imbedded development routines described here were selected because although they are essential to developing business leaders, they were derived from sports team's best practices. They've also been field-tested by extremely busy managers in my Mission Unreasonable Projects. I have witnessed the significant impact that can occur when you make these routines the cornerstone of your organization's leadership development process.

P1/PREPARE	
Principle: Periodically practice basics or foundational skills of your role or profession	**JIDR:** Quarterly study of leadership basics Grounding for Greatness Meetings designed for skill practice

Elite performers in sports routinely refine basic skills to prepare for athletic competition. Tennis players keep working on their backhand strokes. Baseball pitchers refine their throwing mechanics. Hockey players practice skating techniques. Refining basics never stops over the course of a sports career that might span several decades.

What's the significance of preparing and refining basics when it comes to developing business leaders? The assumption seems to be, "Experienced managers have mastered leadership fundamentals, and they have more important things on their plate than to waste time practicing basics." However, this unwritten rule doesn't apply when the goal is to develop elite managers.

In the Learning-While-Working Process, P1/Prepare is designed to accomplish two objectives. The first objective is to replace free-form basics with well-defined basics. The second objective is to create a rhythm for the ongoing refinement of leadership basics over the course of every manager's career.

Quarterly study of leadership basics

The most time-consuming set-up activity for installing the Learning-While-Working Process involves creating a comprehensive list of leadership prerequisites The key word here is "leadership." We're not including the technical aspects of the job, but putting a laser-like focus on facets of leadership. To streamline my clients' efforts to compose their own list, I share a framework with three categories: thinking skills, communication skills, and work-process skills:

Figure 8.2 — A Framework of Basic Skills for Being an Elite Leader

Thinking Skills	Communication Skills	Work Processes
• Recognizing Assumptions • Taking Personal Accountability • Designing Meeting Formats • Diagnosing Teamwork Breakdowns • Thinking Strategically • Prioritizing Goals • Managing Time • Thinking Creatively	• Public Speaking • Listening • Raising Issues • Meeting Facilitation • Sharing Performance-Based Feedback • Enrolling Change Collaborators • Empathic Listening • Delegating • Coaching for Accountability	• Decision-Making • Debriefing • Problem Solving • Action-Planning • Designing Meetings • Forming Teams • Brainstorming/Idea Generation

Unfortunately, these basic leadership skills are those where we commonly accept the compromise of "competence is good enough." Skills such as conducting meetings, listening, speaking, and debriefing, may seem mundane. But let's face it, aren't these the skills we perform for the better part of every day while operating a business?

This comprehensive list of leadership basics becomes the menu from which a management team selects skill sets to focus on and refine in a given quarter, and throughout the year. Over a period of years, most of these basics get practiced, and eventually they resurface, and require an additional round of refinement. Notice this rhythm suggests a best principle: leadership basics always get refined.

Turning mundane meetings into valuable skill-practice occasions

Meetings are all too often thought of as a necessary evil that interferes with getting the real work done. If you heard this sentiment, would you and your team be singing a chorus of "Amen?"

All too often, the very thought of attending another meeting gives rise to a big, bored sigh, rather than an enthusiastic expectation of engagement, purpose, and meaning.

There is nothing inherently wrong with meetings. The problem is that too much free-form conversation occurs, instead of highly-skilled thinking and communication exchanges. The most compelling rationale to repeatedly hone leadership basics comes when such fundamental skills are lacking among meeting participants.

To begin to transform meeting effectiveness, we start by shifting our mindset about the value of meetings. If all there is at work, is time to get better, business leaders need to place a premium value on meeting time. Meetings can no longer be regarded as an intrusion that keeps real work from getting done. Instead, meetings must be viewed as the most fertile practice field for galvanizing learning and refining skills. No matter what the format, physical or virtual, meetings can be a place where real work and skill building get done together, and where participants feel focused and energized, instead of bored and drained.

Accountability for meeting quality rests with the parties who co-create the experience—the individuals responsible for running the meeting, as well as participants who create the conversation. Most leaders and meeting participants never receive training in meeting design. They inherit a default meeting template—typically a PowerPoint presentation followed by quick Q&A—suited for exchanging information, but woefully inadequate for skill-building.

Without offering an explanation of meeting design, I will provide you with a succinct three-step template to make any meeting into a skill-building occasion. As a case example, let's take two skills from the leadership prerequisites that are vital to productive meetings: public speaking and performance-based feedback.

While public speaking is a keystone habit for leaders, most organizations don't establish performance standards or expect constant improvement. Unfortunately, most people never develop a skill-based repertoire of speaking skills to rely on during presentations. So when invited to speak, they talk too fast, use too many "um's," awkwardly read PowerPoint slides, all symptoms commonly referred to as "dying while giving a speech." Meanwhile, audience members suffer from a phenomenon known as "Death by PowerPoint." If you Google search "staying awake during boring speeches," you'll access over a million links offering remedies, like using smart phones as meeting survival gear or drawing caricatures of co-workers. Since speakers receive little or no constructive feedback, this death scene will continue to play out in countless meeting rooms throughout the world.

Paul, one of my coaching clients, heads up the prestigious Wal-Mart account for a global consumer products manufacturer. He had just given the most important speech of his career to the company's board of directors. When I asked him how it went, he said, "I didn't get any specific feedback. Just the usual 'Nice job,' comments." Pausing for a moment, I said, "You just played in a championship game without bothering to take video footage to study afterward." Paul was initially perplexed by my remark. He was at a loss to figure out how to inject and ensure feedback in such a meeting. In his company, speeches and presentations, which take up the bulk of meeting time, are a feedback-free zone.

Since one of Paul's goals is to become an orchestrator of excellent habits, I coached him to make a mindset shift—seeing every meeting as a skill-building occasion. We then mapped out three changes in the meeting design to cover skill practice related to public speaking and feedback.

Pre-speech setup: All speakers describe a specific skill they'll be practicing in their upcoming presentation, as well as the evaluation criteria audience members should use in offering feedback. For example, any speaker might choose to practice skills like organizing a speech, using vocal variety, crafting a persuasive message, employing nonverbal gestures, and telling engaging stories. Feedback criteria for these skills can be found in Internet searches or consulting with in-house trainers. A one-stop shop for feedback criteria covering a range of speaking skills is *The Competent Speaker* manual available from Toastmasters International at http://www.toastmasters.org.

During the presentation: Each meeting participant listens to the presentation to grasp the speaker's message, and writes down feedback.

Post-presentation: After the presentation, each speaker listens to feedback from a designated evaluator, who shares strengths, weaknesses, and suggestions for improvement. The speaker summarizes the feedback, and indicates changes he or she will practice in future presentations. The other meeting participants pass on their written feedback to each speaker.

Redesigning meetings as an occasion for skill building sends a message to every speaker: Winging it is prohibited. Every presentation is an opportunity to practice improving their speaking skills. No one is permitted to plateau.

Audience members are no longer passive listeners who tolerate speakers practicing ineffective behaviors. Instead, their role is to provide helpful feedback to speakers, learn the performance criteria for various speaking skills, and improve the quality of their feedback skills. Over time, the team watches in amazement as their peers transform their performance as speakers. Everyone gains small wins through this process.

Grounding for Greatness

P1/Prepare includes a daily warm-up routine called a Grounding for Greatness, to reestablish the rhythm to engage with the deliberate practice opportunities ahead. It is similar to a sports team reviewing game day assignments in their locker room before the real competition starts. A Grounding for Greatness serves several purposes:

- To acknowledge learning as a goal to pursue throughout the work day.
- To instill the sense of confidence needed to face challenging deliberate practice opportunities that arise during the day.
- To provide practice in the core skills needed for engaging in deliberate practice.

A Grounding for Greatness is led by managers who've been trained to function in the role of head coach. To get the meeting started, two participants each take on the role of deliberate practitioner. They describe their deliberate practice plan for the day by addressing three questions: *What is the specific learning goal for today's practice? What practice situations will be available? What methods will be used for eliciting feedback on the skill practice?*

The head coach or any member of the group can ask questions like:

How can you revise your skill improvement goal so you feel an edge of apprehension, but don't feel overwhelmed? If you can't arrange for feedback from a team member, what are the criteria you can observe in assessing your own performance?

The designated head coach troubleshoots any potential obstacles that might keep the deliberate practitioners from completing their plans. Excellent troubleshooting questions include:

What circumstances could arise where you'll choose to forgo your skill practice plan? What reasons could you possibly use to legitimize your choice to give up on your plan? If circumstances interfere with your original plan for practice, what's your backup plan?

These questions are taken seriously because at the next Grounding for Greatness, deliberate practitioners will report the actual results of their deliberate practice efforts.

Notice the profound small wins made possible by this daily startup ritual. How would you feel starting every workday knowing you belong to an organization whose members are constantly empowered to discover their full potential? Team members show plenty of confidence when leaving a Grounding for Greatness. And the team's employee engagement ratings soar off the charts.

Practice Drill: Instilling Urgency to Transform Meetings Into Skill-Building Occasions

In this practice drill, you'll be taking the initial steps in transforming the quality of your organization's meetings. This transformation has two parts. You will first eliminate the free-form basics that produce a poor, or even pathetic, meeting quality. Afterwards, you will install a set of well-defined leadership skills to spark inspired, fully engaged meeting participation.

Assess the quality of your meetings

Be ruthlessly honest in answering the following questions:

- If your competition saw your senior management meeting on YouTube, how would they react? Would they be intimidated by a display of skillful conversation, or be emboldened to compete after witnessing the poor substance of your meeting?

- After watching your team in action, would a candidate for an executive position want to accept or refuse a job offer from your company?

- What are the most egregious free form basics present at your meetings, which damage the quality of your team's experience and the effectiveness of their collaboration?

Spell out leadership basics

If your answers to the preceding questions are unsettling, develop a list of basic leadership skills specifically for your organization. Use my earlier framework (Figure 8.2: A Framework of Basic Skills for Being an Elite Leader) to organize these basics into the categories of thinking skills, communication skills, and work processes.

Give your list closer scrutiny. Which skills or processes does your team perform as free-form basics? Which of these have well-defined processes? Form small study groups to research leadership best practices to replace your current version of free-form basics.

Refine basics during team meetings

To provide practice opportunities, require each meeting facilitator to review the agenda to determine which items require using basic skills like problem solving, idea generation, or decision-making. Be sure your team spells out the proper how-to steps for performing any of these skills or processes before you even practice.

Videotape meetings for self-study

Duke University's basketball Coach Mike Kryzyzewski videotapes timeout huddles to see if his entire team is being fully present to the conversation, and to review the quality of what's being said. When Bill Walsh coached the San Francisco 49'ers, he recorded team meetings to ensure his assistant coaches, who would change from year to year, were teaching in a consistent fashion. How will you use videotape as a quality-control method or skill-building technology, to improve the quality of your team meetings?

Key takeaway idea

P1/Prepare by refining basics is the foundation for the entire Learning-While-Working Process. It establishes standards that apply to practicing, performing, perfecting, and publicizing. If you permit free-form basics to serve as implicit performance standards, then job-imbedded development opportunities triggered by all the 5Ps will amount to practicing ineffective behaviors.

P2/PRACTICE	
Principle: Stage deliberate practice in the midst of real work	**JIDR:** Re-Do bad habits Instant practice protocal

When P-2/Practice happens in business, it doesn't occur as a designated block of hours each day where work activities stop, and everyone assembles for team practice like they do in sports. Instead, individuals create their own job-imbedded development routines by deliberately practicing in the midst of doing their day's tasks.

Instant practice protocol for self-coaching

Instant practice protocol is a tool for self-debriefing or critiquing after deliberate practice occurs during your normal job assignments. This approach builds upon the research done on self-regulation, pioneered by Barry J. Zimmerman and his colleagues at the City University of New York.[1] Each occasion of instant practice protocol amounts to taking moments for reflection in the midst of getting work done, in order to accomplish the following three steps:

Step 1: Predetermine an improvement goal: Every task at work becomes an opportunity for building skills by focusing on various facets of performance. Ask yourself questions like: What do I want to convey in this interaction? What kind of emotional tone do I want to create? What kind of value-added performance can I offer to a team member or customer? What would raising my skill proficiency look like?

Step 2: Mindful reflection: In the midst of performing a task, observe your effectiveness in executing your improvement goals. Gauge how well your actions measure up to established performance criteria for the skill being practiced. Notice the impact of your practice on customers and team members.

Step 3: Post-practice debriefing: Review your entire practice effort to make an overall self-assessment. Address the question: What was my desired improvement when I set out to practice, and how well was it accomplished? Aim to slightly surpass your own personal best performance in each practice round.

Coaching interaction: Injecting valuable coaching to a customary fact-finding interview

I frequently use instant practice protocol. In the following example, I use it in a client interview for customizing an upcoming seminar. My typical pre-seminar phone interview is purely a fact-finding mission. I want to know about audience composition, if there are organizational changes in the works, or key messages the senior executives would like me to reinforce. In step one of instant practice protocol, I set my improvement goal—to add value for my interviewee by offering him my coaching expertise. I ask this personal question: *What task do you want to accomplish, that, although you have the know-how to do it, you never seem to have sufficient time?*

That question ignited a coaching exchange with Nick, a home improvement store manager, who responded, "I never have time to coach and develop my department managers because I get sucked in by the daily haphazards of being a store manager."

I am struck by Nick's choice of words, which convey his sense of being a victim of unrelenting distractions. In my own self-reflection (*step 2 of instant practice protocol*), I'm thinking: Nick assumes the nature of his job is to encounter endless interruptions. Sounds like a victim mindset. This is an ideal time to introduce coaching.

"Nick, getting sucked in is a choice."

Nick's silence shows he is caught off-guard by my interpretation of his situation, which indicates he is accountable for making a choice.

"Are you open to my coaching?"

Nick's "Okay," was delivered with a what-have-I gotten-myself-into tone.

"Nick, what actions are you choosing to take, or avoid taking, that undermine having time for coaching your team members?"

"I probably don't delegate enough."

"Give me examples where you might have delegated, but chose not to do so."

"When technology breaks down, I communicate with the vendors to get it fixed. When there's a staff scheduling problem, I solve it."

"What payoffs are you choosing to gain by not delegating?"

"I do things better and faster," Nick answers. "Besides, I don't want to take extra time to fix things if someone else mishandles the situation."

"So you don't have time to teach your assistant managers to solve problems because you're busy solving their problems for them?"

"Now I see what you mean by having a choice," says Nick.

As I again pause to take stock of what's happening (*step 2 of instant practice protocol*), I notice Nick is open to being coached, and decide to offer empathy for his situation. "Nick, as store manager, you think your top priority is to get things to run smoothly, and therefore the best way is to depend on yourself to handle problems."

Nick concurs. "Either I do it, or face having to clean up someone else's mess."

"I understand you're committed to avoiding messes in the short-term. And what are the long-term costs if you continue to avoid delegating?"

Nick insists, "I need to be a hands-on manager for the time being. I'd be irresponsible if I let people make decisions who aren't ready. When my managers screw up, my boss will come down on me."

Once again, I take a few seconds to consider what to say next (*step 2 of instant practice protocol*). I'm thinking: While I've asked several times, Nick still doesn't acknowledge the long-term implications. I need to offer stronger medicine.

I resume coaching by asking, "This one-size-fits-all-employees form of micromanaging is equivalent to committing theft."

"Theft? I don't know what you mean."

"Your job is to develop department managers to perform tasks and make decisions appropriate to their role. But you're actually doing the challenging parts of their job, while you're being paid a boss's salary."

Nick pauses for five seconds, which probably felt like five minutes. "I never realized the financial costs you've described. I really don't have any choice but to delegate."

Sensing Nick is ready to choose to take accountability for his micromanaging, our conversation moves smoothly into problem-solving mode. Nick agrees to test his assumptions about his managers' capabilities, and keep a log to record his basis for choosing whether to delegate or micromanage. Tracking his deliberations requires Nick to make mindful choices.

After finishing the call, I take five minutes for self-debriefing (*step 3 of instant practice protocol*). I jot down notes about what I did well. My planned question to direct Nick to explore one of his plateaus worked perfectly to shift the conversation from fact-finding to coaching. A turning point in the conversation came when I provoked Nick's mindset shift by describing micromanaging as tantamount to theft. I also noted one area where I could improve. I should have asked Nick to explain, in his own words, the valuable insights he gleaned from this coaching session, to ensure he takes ownership for generating them.

The small wins weren't confined to a single practice drill. Three weeks later during the actual seminar, Nick related his enormous success with delegating. I couldn't have asked for a better testimonial to affirm the value of my tools for Nick's fellow store managers. From this episode of instant practice protocol, I raised my standards for future customizing interviews.

Taking a mulligan—Re-Do ineffective behaviors

During friendly games among rank amateurs, golfers generously give each other a chance to do over a bad shot, like driving a ball into a water hazard. This ritual affording golfers the chance to practice the instant after making a mistake is called "taking a mulligan." Unfortunately, great learning opportunities are being missed because there is no business version of a mulligan for seasoned managers, who are expected to know how to perform basic tasks. When team members practice ineffectively, allowing mulligans is extremely beneficial, and not offering them is a huge disservice.

Does this sound like elite leadership development—saying nothing at the time, and then commenting about someone's bad habits a year later in a peer 360 review or performance appraisal? Another way to improve ineffective behavior is to instantly give constructive feedback, even if it's in the midst of a staff meeting. Feedback is a much better response than silence, but the misbehaving individual misses a wonderful opportunity to instantly practice to improve his or her performance.

My version for giving and taking mulligans in leadership development is called *Re-Do*. This P2/Practice strategy is designed to trigger immediate practice, stopping an ineffective behavior and simultaneously replacing it with a more skillful response.

> *A Re-Do makes it safe to publicly take*
> *accountability for bad habits in the most powerful*
> *way possible—instantly changing ineffective*
> *behaviors in front of team members.*

Making Re-Do into a game

When I first met Scott, a CEO in the software industry, he fit the stereotype of a know-it-all leader. However, Scott cared deeply about developing an elite group of senior managers. Scott wasn't the only team member with a glaring weakness. His colleagues' interpersonal flaws were on full display during meetings, but were tolerated without comment.

Scott stepped up as a leader by challenging his team to change their ineffective behaviors. As the leader, he went first. Scott requested his colleagues call for a "Re-Do" in response to two of his bad habits that usually appeared during strategic conversations. First, Scott often responded to team members' input on strategic issues with a condescending tone and harsh critiques. At the Re-Do signal, Scott was required to stop his criticism, and start practicing open-minded inquiry into his colleagues' reasoning for suggesting a strategic move. He prepared several scripted inquiries: "What's your basis for reaching that conclusion?" and "What short-term and long-term value does your idea bring to our business?" The second habit that needed work was Scott's tendency to dominate the conversation when it came time to tout his own ideas. Upon receiving the Re-Do signal, Scott switched from his long-winded monologue style to inviting questions designed to draw out his colleagues' strategic thinking. He asked questions such as: "What information gaps do you see that I haven't taken into consideration? How would you connect the dots differently? How could we improve on my ideas?"

Now Scott's entire team employs the Re-Do drill. As each senior manager sits down at the boardroom table, he or she displays a name tent with a colorful phrase to capture the ineffective behavior they've agreed to change, and, in turn, be called out for a Re-Do. Scott's reads, "Smartest Guy in the Room." Rebecca, an operations manager, writes, "Passing the Buck," which refers to her tendency to blame unfavorable circumstances for missed results. Walter chooses, "Hot Head," because whenever he wants colleagues to take a problem seriously, he uses angry outbursts to intimidate them.

If you're thinking, "That kind of openness to challenge each other could never happen on my senior management team," then think again. If Scott's management team refuses to challenge each other to improve, they will continue to criticize, blame, and intimidate.

What varieties of ineffective behaviors occur among the members of your management team? Can you really tolerate *not* having the degree of openness that permits instant deliberate practice? Because *you get what you tolerate.*

You get what you tolerate.

Accepting the need for behavior change as normal, even desirable, among team members, through using a Re-Do, creates a series of small wins. It makes your colleagues not only teammates, but your partners. And because it does away with pretense, everyone is more at ease admitting their own need for improvement, and they cooperate more fully when working on skill-building together. Re-Do gets big results when practiced as a playful game. Everyone's flaws are on the table in full display. Everyone is taking risks, being vulnerable, and building significant trust. *Re-Do acknowledges incompetence as an integral part of growth, making the meeting room a safe place to change and grow.*

Practice Drill: Make it Safe to Re-Do Ineffective Behaviors

Most organizations lack a safe method like Re-Do to legitimize a process for challenging ineffective behaviors.

Customize your own Re-Do

Implement the following three steps to set up the conditions for a successful Re-Do process with your team members:

1. What ineffective behavior do you agree should have a standing order for Re-Do? If you need a jumpstart to address this question, common Re-Do's include:

    *   When you're sparing with compliments in reviewing a team member's exemplary work,
    *   When you don't stick to the core topic of a conversation, but take the conversation off on a tangent by saying whatever is on your mind,
    *   When you fail to clarify and agree on the purpose of a phone call, and everyone discovers later they're not on the same page.

2. What would you write on your name tent to describe your own Re-Do? Your moniker can either communicate the bad habit you want to stop or the replacement response. Let's say you've tolerated being micromanaged by permitting your boss to continually make decisions that are really your responsibility. Your moniker could be "Willing Accomplice" to indicate the ineffective behavior you want to change. Another moniker might be "Braveheart" to call forth the courage you'll need when you point out your boss hasn't assumed his/her responsibility to help develop your ability to make sound decisions. Coming up with creative and even humorous monikers evokes playful engagement by the entire team when calling for a Re-Do.

3. What replacement response would you script for yourself when you're called out for the Re-Do on your name tent? Think of a more effective action, or write down helpful phrases you could use. Many times, the best Re-do response is silence. Instead of the usual putdowns, bragging, excuses, or sarcasm—just stop using ineffective behaviors.

Key takeaway idea

As a team leader, it's your job to be the first one to generate a game-like approach for Re-Do. Everyone will feel more comfortable once they see their boss accept being called out for a Re-Do by direct reports with good humor and then commit to fix his or her own flaws and shortcomings.

P3/PERFORM	
Principle: Declare game-on situations when there's high impact on business results or learning outcomes	**JIDR:** Specify vital work processes Transfer of training

In my interview with Greg Olson, former catcher for the Atlanta Braves, he shared his perspective on why the team had an incredible winning streak.

> *"I honestly believe the main reason we went to the 1991 World Series, which began the streak of making the playoffs for 14 straight years, was a players-only meeting at the All-Star break. Sid Bream and Terry Pendleton were our team leaders who had playoff experience. We were a young club at the time, about nine games behind the league-leading Dodgers. Terry maintained we had the right talent and the right preparation from our coaches to pose a threat to the Dodgers. He convinced us we needed to focus on giving*

our best performance and cut down on mental mistakes. When we walked over the white foul lines, we recited a mantra—'Between the white lines, we're the best team.' We went on to win eight out of nine games, and the rest is history."[2]

Crossing the foul lines was the signal or trigger to prompt the Atlanta Braves to declare a game-on condition for their upcoming performance. In the Learning-While-Working Process, P3/Perform designates a slice of time at work as "game-on," making it worthy of an extra-special quality of performance. The word "perform" itself carries valuable connotations. The task at hand becomes 1) worth preparing for, 2) worth fully focusing on, since an important audience is watching, and 3) worth critiquing, so performance improves for the next game-on occasion.

What is at stake in a game-on period? Game-on status might be assigned to high-impact events like quarterly strategic planning meetings (since an organization's future direction takes shape there), performance appraisal conversations (when plans for a year's worth of professional development are being formulated), key account sales meetings (when a single customer accounts for a large percentage of total revenue), and returning from a training program (when the return on investment in the training is determined).

Just like the Atlanta Braves crossing the foul lines on a baseball field, every job can be broken down into game-on periods. Let's examine job-imbedded routines perfectly suited for two specific game-on situations: 1) during effective problem-solving conversations, and 2) transferring what is learned during classroom training to the workplace.

Replacing free-form basics with a definite process for problem solving

Free-form basics have no place in game-on situations. Rene Fritz, founder of Chief Executive Forum groups for mid-size business CEOs employs the following 20-10-10-5 problem-solving method:

Figure 8.3 — Chief Executive Forum's Problem-Solving Format

Steps	Actions	Length of Time
1. Describe the problem	The presenter lays out a pressing problem. No interruptions are permitted.	20 minutes
2. Probe for missing details	The rest of the CEOs take turns asking questions to clarify the missing details	10 minutes
3. Offer solutions	The rest of the CEOs share their own experiences with similar problems, along with their analysis of potential solutions	10 minutes
4. Promises for action	The presenter summarizes key insights and makes promises to initiate solutions	5 minutes

Why does the Chief Executive Forum impose such a precise routine on its senior executive members? The routine ensures problem-solving gets treated as a game-on occasion. CEOs can't afford to waste time at these sessions on lightweight problems, or have members going off on a tangent. The problem-solving structure details roles and time lines. The 20-10-10-5 format calls for specific thinking and communication skills in a rhythmic progression: **attentive listening→ questioning for clarity→ offering well-reasoned solutions→ summarizing learning points**.

Transfer of training as a game-on situation

Senior executives who love efficiency often misjudge the relative contributions of training and development in building leadership capabilities. They hope a few days of solid training will be sufficient to impart new leadership skills. But training, typically a classroom course or online self-study program, is only the resource for acquiring know-how. The job-imbedded development routines implemented after training are the real game-on occasions. When trainees return to work, they need to practice new skills, make mistakes, receive feedback, and develop self-confidence, so their new leadership skills become second nature. To bring out an individual's full leadership capacity, training and job-imbedded development must be an integrated process.

Based in Watsonville, California, Driscoll's is not only a world-class supplier and marketer of berries, but a superb environment for growing elite talent. The epitome of their people development efforts is Driscoll's Leadership Institute (DLI) for high-performing leaders. DLI consists of five two- to three-day meetings per year. But the real return on investment comes from a rich variety of job-imbedded development routines done by trainees between sessions.

"We've always been a homegrown business," CEO Miles Reiter told me. "Our management team realized not only did we lack bench strength, but we ourselves were in over our head in attempting to lead this company." At first, I was struck by this brutally honest self-assessment. Then I remembered humility is one of Driscoll's core values. Reiter described the original DLI plan. "We didn't want a flavor of the month with isolated leadership training classes. So we ruled out sending people to university education classes. We saw value in conducting a year-long classroom training that was combined with experiences to reinforce key take-away ideas back on the job."[3]

Here's a sample of the developmental experiences forming the rhythm for Driscoll's Leadership Institute (DLI):

- *Working in a customer setting.* This is not a casual site visit. As the kickoff to DLI, and to emphasize customer focus as their most important leadership competency, participants work a week alongside produce personnel in their top customers' stores.

- *Individual development plan.* DLI participants work with their managers to identify areas for building leadership capacity. The plan becomes a living document, which changes throughout the year as new opportunities to utilize leadership skills emerge. Participants seek phone coaching with the DLI support team to keep their development plan on track.

- *Developmental opportunities.* DLI graduates practice skills they learned in training in specially-crafted experiences such as job shadowing, representing Driscoll's at industry events, working with an accountability group, and serving on community boards.

- *Monthly mentoring sessions*: DLI alumni serve as mentors for the current DLI participants.

- *Small group assignment:* Groups of three to five participants work together on short-term projects that require them to apply program content. For example, teams observe and report on examples of behaviors that define Driscoll's values, as well as behaviors that are in conflict with the values.

- *Publicizing:* DLI participants share what they learn with work teams and their bosses. To solidify their own learning, they all have the opportunity to prepare a training module to teach others.

- *Annual 180-degree or 360-degree peer review:* Feedback from peers helps DLI leaders assess the impact of their behavior changes on team members and cross-functional peers.

- *Analysis of strategic initiatives.* Teams take three months to analyze a strategic initiative from Driscoll's strategic plan. They assess progress made, identify problems, and recommend ways to enhance the effectiveness of the initiative. Finally, they present these findings to the executive team.

This rich list of developmental opportunities takes plenty of time for the participants, but the intrinsic value of the DLI training goes without question by Driscoll's top brass. "Our people are our biggest strategic advantage," said Miles Reiter. "If we didn't challenge ourselves to get better, we shouldn't even have bothered to start this business."

Practice Drill: Up-Leveling Free-Form Basics to Game-On Performances

You can elevate any activity's significance to game-on stature by naming it to evoke certain behaviors and requiring your team spell out the steps before they can start doing it.

Name activities to evoke game-on readiness

One of the best ways to signal game-on situations is to name processes to evoke inspired performance. Hewlett Packard coined the phrase, Management by Wandering Around (MBWA), to signal managers to use daily check-in meetings to practice an array of skills like listening, giving feedback, coaching, and problem-solving. In working with sales organizations, I use the term, "Sales Calls Customers Would Pay For," to bring added significance to less glamorous activities of pre-call planning, or post-call debriefing that surround a key account call.

What are the seemingly mundane tasks where you can employ naming to trigger game-on readiness and leverage opportunities for learning and skill-building?

Institute certification calls

In sports, players demonstrate their prowess in executing the game plan before they earn a role in the starting lineup. Preparation is a pre-requisite to earn significant playing time in big games. If players aren't ready to execute the game plan with excellence, they take a seat on the bench. Why not require business leaders to demonstrate their readiness to play major roles in high-impact game-on situations?

In a certification call, the meeting facilitator checks on both individual and group readiness to adhere to performance standards before embarking on a task/process. If the participants can't describe the key steps for executing a given task/process, they are declared unqualified to perform it and begin a remedial study period before getting another chance for certification.

From your list of leadership basics, decide which processes are so vital they merit a certification call. Consider processes like decision-making, problem-solving, idea generation, debriefing a key account sales call, staging a recovery with a top customer, and setting strategic priorities.

Key takeaway idea

To derail the default organizational tempo of cut-to-the-chase efficiency, you can deploy evocative language and certification rituals to keep their team mindful of opportunities that require excellent performance.

P4/PERFECT	
Principle: Debrief to improve just-completed processes	**JIDR:** Debriefing protocols Assumption collecting

P4/Perfect is all about improving through debriefing. Most companies end meetings by debriefing with a casual, "How do you think that went?" discussion. It's another example of a misplaced free-form basic used in what should be a game-on situation. In addition, participants confuse "debriefing" with a summary of action outcomes. Debriefing involves critiquing the just-completed process, whether it be a meeting, a six-month project, or an individual's performance of a single task.

The U.S. Army's After Action Review (AAR) is the gold standard for perfecting a work process once a task is completed.[4] With AAR, discussion centers on four sequential questions:

1. What did we set out to do? (describing performance standards)

2. What actually happened? (assessing strengths and weaknesses)

3. Why did it happen? (diagnosing cause and effect)

4. What are we going to do next time? (brainstorming improvements)

Outside the Army, many groups start their reviews at diagnosis (question 3), assuming they can omit prior debriefing steps without problems. But agreement on both the standards to be met (question 1), as well as actual performance (question 2), is essential to prevent endless debates about the facts. The Army recommends allocating the first 25 percent of time spent in AAR to cover the first two assessment questions, 25 percent to the third, and 50 percent to the fourth.

Assumption collecting—a debriefing for strategic conversations

Without anyone realizing it, assumptions shape a company's future. Assumption collecting is a valuable way for a business to make sure it isn't being restricted by blind spots. How does a senior management team become aware of their blind spots? Revealing strategic assumptions is a vital skill that deserves to be practiced frequently.

My clients use assumption collecting in P4/Perfect, as a deliberate practice opportunity. Here's how this type of debriefing works. One meeting participant's role is the assumption collector who listens carefully to the conversation, and compiles a list of expressed, or implied, nature-of-the-business assumptions ("We're a family-owned business, and don't need lots of formal procedures for training and development"), and strategic assumptions ("To continue being the undisputed low-price leader by our target customers, we must staff our business to control labor costs").

The P4/Perfect trigger signals for a debriefing period during the last ten to fifteen minutes of a meeting. The assumption collector selects two or three assumptions from his/her list to undergo closer scrutiny. Along with reading each assumption, the assumption collector calls for two votes: "Show of hands if you judge the assumption to be factually accurate and effective at producing results. Show of hands if you consider the assumption to be factually incorrect or ineffective at producing desired results." After each vote, group members explain the reasoning behind their assessment. Assumptions that deserve deeper scrutiny become an important agenda item at a future team meeting.

Before you worry about losing ten minutes at every meeting to scrutinize assumptions, consider the potential value of practicing this complex skill. In its early years, McDonald's made the assumption: Customers want speedy service, which requires using a limited menu of burgers, thick shakes, and fries. In contrast to McDonald's current robust menu, it's hard to believe executives held this assumption during the startup years. In fact, Tyson, the world's largest supplier of chicken (which of course wasn't on the menu), served the role of assumption collector for McDonald's. Their elite sales team revealed the mistaken assumptions about menu size and speed of service that paved the way for a more expanded menu as well as a blockbuster product, Chicken McNuggets. The better question is: How can your senior leaders afford not to practice identifying assumptions that can shape your company's destiny?

> *"Curiosity is life. Assumption is death."*
> —**Mike Parker, CEO, Nike**

 Practice Drill: Instilling Vigilance to Lock in New Debriefing Habits

Most management teams struggle to establish a debriefing protocol to close a meeting. It's no wonder. We're so accustomed to finishing meetings armed with an action plan specifying roles and time lines for accomplishing the next steps. With the clock ticking, it takes unwavering commitment to allocate even ten minutes to debrief the meeting process or the performance quality of the just-completed group interaction. This practice drill will enable you to implement certain measures to insure debriefing becomes an indispensible conclusion to every meeting.

Install triggering mechanisms

As an orchestrator of elite habits, your job is to install triggering mechanisms to ensure that meetings reliably conclude with an effective debriefing. Consider these questions in formulating your triggers:

- What roles can you assign meeting attendees to ensure debriefing happens regularly? Consider rotating the role of debriefing facilitator— the person who keeps the group on track to allot adequate time for debriefing, reviews the group's debriefing protocol, and then facilitates the group's critique of the just-completed meeting process.

- Besides an assumption collector, what other content and conduct would be valuable for observers to track with the goal of improving performance? To polish public speaking skills, Toastmasters clubs appoint an "ah-counter" to record the number of filler phrases speakers use during their presentations.

- What signs, sounds, or physical stimuli can you use to trigger a debriefing period so you always remember to finish a meeting with rigorous debriefing? After performing death-defying feats at an air show, the Navy's Blue Angels start their debriefing by each pilot saying, "Good to be here."

Key takeaway idea

If you want to have consistent debriefing, it must become a habit. In the beginning, you will need to rely on triggering mechanisms to launch debriefing. Gradually, your team members will come to look forward to the small wins—the learning, skill building, recognition—all derived from debriefing. Eventually, no one will consider bypassing the opportunity for debriefing.

P5/PUBLICIZE	
Principle: After a learning experience, ask, "Who else could benefit?"	**JIDR:** Distiller's report Online sharing vehicles

P4/Perfect and P5/Publicize flow together effortlessly. Debriefing allows team members to discover and recapitulate key learning points. Why not spread the learning to a broader sweep of contacts? Thanks to technology, publicizing learning to a small group, or hundreds of people, can take place in mere minutes. Make it a habit to reflect on the question, "Who else might benefit from the learning that just took place?" It will be a win-win situation for everyone.

Here's how P5/Publicize works in Mission Unreasonable Projects. For each group meeting, or individual coaching session, one person takes the role of distiller. The distiller's role calls for participating in the actual meeting, while also being a selective editor who records the group's key learnings. Afterwards, the distiller takes no more than fifteen minutes to compose an e-mail capturing the fresh insights and informational gems. Distillers' reports are like a blog, usually 200 to 300 words. The best reports contain juicy tidbits like practical tips, mindset shifts, bringing awareness to previous blind spots, and a list of the strengths and weaknesses exhibited in the meeting.

Here's an example of a valuable insight shared by Joan, a vice president of sales operations, in her distiller's report after an individual coaching session, which she e-mailed to her six-person senior management team:

> Reflecting on the coaching session today, I noticed what may be a common theme with our group. In setting our individual performance goals for the year, we use generalities, and shy away from the potential discomfort that could come from clearly declaring an observable and measurable goal for behavior change. Vague behavioral descriptions provide us with an escape route from accountability.

Contrast the forthright candor and vulnerability in Joan's distiller's report with the typical humdrum summary of action steps. Distiller's reports are a much deeper and more revealing communication that describes personal insights, intellectual discoveries, and new bits of learning.

Besides e-mailing a distiller's report, publicizing can take additional forms:

- *LISTSERV or web portal*: To increase ROI from a major meeting, attendees use technology to publicize their implementation plans and actual results achieved.

- *Designated editor*. On a monthly or quarterly basis, choose a team member to circulate a list of best books to read, or to send links for relevant articles or blogs.

- *In-house team blog.* Post a provocative blog with the intent of stimulating fresh thinking in responses by team members.

- *Social media affinity groups.* LinkedIn offers a chance to communicate with peers with similar interests who might benefit from your team's key learning points.

- *Videotape.* After a conference, create an online collection of videotapes that communicate key messages and actionable ideas for colleagues who didn't attend.

Practice Drill: Maintain a Log of Accumulated Learning

In this practice drill, you will develop practices to help retain new insights and knowledge acquired from communications triggered by P5/Publicizing.

Keep your own log of distiller's reports

Distiller's reports are the most efficient, and most frequent, form of publicizing. Keep a log of the cumulative learning expressed in your own distiller's reports. Record the most useful ideas you glean from your colleague's submissions to add to your records. Your log is evidence of your continual growth towards becoming an elite performer.

Team blog

Create an in-house blog where team members share their emerging insights and practical tips, with their colleagues. Be sure to share lessons learned from successes and failures.

Key takeaway idea

Publicizing generates lots of small wins. When a blogger takes a minute to distill a learning experience in writing, he or she often will conceive new insights and reinforce the original learning so it becomes stored in memory. In turn, blog readers might derive solutions to a problem from a colleague they would never have considered to be a potential resource.

Committing to the Learning-While-Working Process

Measuring efficiency and effectiveness

Two fundamental concerns—time-efficiency and quantifiable results—must be resolved before a leader will commit to take on the Learning-While-Working Process. Business leaders wonder how long the various job-imbedded development routines actually take out of the work day. They realize that any work process improvement needs to be measured to assess how well it is being implemented along with its impact on performance.

To illustrate the time-efficiency of the Learning-While-Working Process, here is a rundown of rough time requirements necessary to accomplish various job-imbedded development routines:

Figure 8.4 — Typical Time Expended for Job-Imbedded Development Routines

Checklist of Job Imbedded Development Routines		
✓	Instant practice protocol	5-10 minutes for self-debriefing
✓	Re-do of ineffective behavior	30 seconds to 2 minutes
✓	Grounding for Greatness daily warm-up	20 minutes
✓	Debrief a staff meeting	10-15 minutes
✓	Assumption collecting votes	10 minutes
✓	Prepare a distiller's report and send e-mails to publicize key insights	15 minutes
✓	Redesign an update meeting to incorporate skill-building drills	Periodic 5-6 minute feedback exchanges

After a period for getting acquainted with these new routines, team members easily take responsibility to initiate a Re-Do, engage in instant practice protocol, stage a Grounding for Greatness, or publicize their latest learning tips. Eventually, these routines occur so automatically, team members would never consider reverting back to their old ways. Leadership development is a daily activity for everyone, whether they are honing their own leadership skills or contributing to a colleague's growth. When responsibility for development is shared, it's more efficient and realistic than when the boss has sole accountability.

A second concern you may have in implementing the Learning-While-Working Process is how to measure the effectiveness of the 5Ps, including the whole integrated process for leadership development. Since there aren't many widely used key performance indicators (KPI) for leadership development, I'll help jump-start your own fresh thinking by suggesting two categories of measurements that matter. The first category measures a group's effectiveness in executing the Learning-While-Working Process and its various job-imbedded development routines:

- Number of deliberate practice hours: Time spent in self-managed activities that incorporate rigorous deliberate practice.

- Percentage of time in "flow" state: The percentage of uninterrupted time spent fully absorbed in high priority work that calls for creative thinking.

- Number of feedback exchanges per week: The number of times each team member receives verbal feedback over the course of a week.

- Publicizing frequency: The number of weekly communications to publicize new learning sent by each team member to others who might benefit.

- Number of Re-Do's: The number of times Re-Dos occur in staff meetings where an individual's well-recognized ineffective behavior is replaced by a more skillful response.

- Number of hours spent coaching/mentoring per week.

The second category takes into account the tangible improvements in leadership capabilities for individual leaders and their direct reports, plus the impact on the entire organization:

- Decrease in marks ranked below acceptable level on 360 peer review evaluation scores.

- Number of team members qualified to perform at the next level of management.

- Number of employees considered emerging talent or high potentials.

- Number of times team members were assigned to lead a major project.

- Turnover of direct reports.

- Percentage of offers accepted by candidates interviewed.

- Improvements in engagement ratings of direct reports and their team members.

- Percentage of direct reports whose high-priority areas for improvement were noticeably better than in their last performance appraisal.

- Percentage of time spent in leadership development activities.

Treat these measurements as potential small wins to motivate sticking with job-imbedded development routines. Frequent small wins insure habits become permanent. The 5Ps of the Learning-While-Working Process become the natural way work gets done.

Rolling out the Learning-While-Working Process

You may also be wondering about the best way to roll out the Learning-While-Working Process for your organization. There is more than one way. Andy Tysler, Vice President of Sales for Deschutes Brewery, made the commitment to be an orchestrator of elite habits with his nationwide sales force.[5] Rather than a full rollout of all 5Ps, Andy decided to introduce select practices. He believes once his team notices the immediate impact of the initial array of best practices, they will be motivated to engage in the full Learning-While-Working Process.

Andy requires his whole team to use Re-Do in their individual development plans (IDPs), which are incorporated into their yearly performance plans. Andy's own plan calls for him to invoke a Re-Do whenever his direct reports try to delegate up a decision they've been trained to make on their own and that is appropriate for their role. One regional manager's IDP invites a Re-Do if he asks a blaming-enhancement question like, "What happened in your market to cause the on-premise draught business to decline?" The Re-Do component of IDPs—both the ineffective behavior to change and the replacement response—get communicated to a region's entire staff. With large territories to cover, Andy's sales managers don't always work with their sales reps. However, the reps team up with co-workers to conduct Re-Do's to help each other improve.

Andy also teams up with sales managers for a "work-with" day in the field, making a series of sales calls together. The day starts with a Grounding for Greatness where Andy and his managers set deliberate practice goals. After each sales call, they return to the car and begin P4/Perfect to scrutinize the quality of the performance that just took place. The final debriefing session summarizes their overall progress and areas to improve. Andy follows up with a written recap of the day, coaching suggestions, and Re-Do habits to practice in his absence. He e-mails a copy to the sales manager's boss, reinforcing the coaching points to emphasize in follow-up support.

Most of Andy's direct reports rapidly made these changes, but a few were slow to get onboard. Recognizing the risk of undertaking any bold innovation, Andy committed to address all obstacles in view of the ultimate payoff—a national sales team saturated with elite performers.

Over a three-year period, Wells Enterprises conducted two versions of the Learning-While-Working Process, one for sales operations managers, and another for the senior sales leaders of its Blue Bunny ice cream business. Their experience demonstrates a compelling case for measures of success produced by years of using job-imbedded development routines.

Blue Bunny committed to revamping its leadership development process because the sales force was competing against two consumer products giants, Nestle (Dreyers, Haagen-Dazs, Edy's ice creams) and Unilever (Ben & Jerry's, Breyers, Klondike ice creams), who not only deliver a quality product, but can out-advertise smaller ice cream manufacturers. As a Midwest company expanding to national distribution, Blue Bunny depended on gaining an advantage from developing superior sales and leadership talent. Mike Crone, Senior Vice President of Sales, describes the situation he faced when he arrived at Wells: "It was clear we lacked the tools and fundamentals to be considered ice cream category consultants for our customers. We sold on passion and enthusiasm, and a true belief in our brand and what we stood for. Retail customers loved us, but did not seek us for their category insights."[6]

The Learning-While-Working Process saturated all facets of the selling, according to Crone. "Our call preparation is light years better due to our deliberate practice rehearsals before a call or presentation. Regularly scheduled 'work-with' coaching days feature debriefings between sales managers and reps. We routinely challenge each other to deliver on agreed-upon accountabilities. Our call debriefs are based on adapting the Navy's Blue Angels' best practices. In short, we have become 'unrecognizable' to our previous selves in our skills and processes. The best part is we did not have to give up our passion and enthusiasm for what we do."

Over eight years, sales doubled, making Blue Bunny the fastest-growing brand in the ice cream and novelty category during that time. New customers include national grocery chains such as Kroger and Safeway, plus regional chains like HEB, Giant Eagle, Winn Dixie, and Publix.

The Learning-While-Working Process sets the stage for dominating competitors in every aspect of talent development. You will out-prepare by constantly revisiting fundamentals, out-practice by capitalizing on job-imbedded development routines, out-perform in game-on situations, and out-learn by excelling in debriefing and publicizing. It's no contest!

CONCLUSION:
CREATING YOUR STORY
WORTH TELLING

In most of my speeches and seminars, there's a point where I must pause and compose myself. I tend to get teary-eyed when audience members relate the stories of their breakthrough insights and actual accomplishments. I feel such deep admiration when a CEO stands up and describes a stretch goal for their management team, which would have previously seemed too incredible to put into words. Or when a manager I coached before the seminar reports impressive results, and everyone in the room listens in awe to his/her remarkable accomplishment.

I get choked up because I know what's at stake for these leaders and their organizations as they display the courage necessary to forgo competent performance and pursue elite standards. In each instance, I'm witnessing a defining moment when someone is saying, in essence, "I'm not willing to let the preordained future simply play out." They are committing themselves to create a story worth telling—and a new, more exciting future.

Most times, a story worth telling arises from looking backward, reviewing the struggles and triumphs, and how it all finally came together. But I'm suggesting for this process to work, that you look forward, envisioning how your quest for elite performance will look once it's realized.

Before you begin, it's useful to take stock of the sources of power you've gained from reading this book. The Leadership Development Game Plan is driven by increased capacity for leadership—the trio of roles you have taken on as a leader: *mindset master, deliberate practitioner,* and *orchestrator of elite habits.*

As a mindset master, your interpretations and resulting choices and actions are no longer driven by a fixed sense of what constitutes unreasonable effort and risk. You are not restricted to setting goals that fit within the safe parameters of your comfort zone. You are free to do things your competitors would never dream of doing, separating yourself from your competition—not for one brilliant year or two, but for your entire leadership tenure.

As a deliberate practitioner, you have a deep understanding of the most effective and efficient way to practice getting better each and every day. You don't have to tolerate hit-or-miss results in improving your skill proficiency, or being stuck at hard-to-master plateaus. Furthermore, since deliberate practice is a keystone habit, it will easily flow into other areas of your life where you exert leadership—your marriage, your parenting, your community service, your friendships.

As an orchestrator of elite habits, you have the power to help your team build capabilities in the midst of getting real work done. Leadership development doesn't occur in classrooms on training days, or in mentoring and coaching sessions alone. It doesn't take a day off. It becomes how you go about your work—all the time.

I invite you to sense the access to leadership power at your disposal when you embrace the roles of mindset master, deliberate practitioner, and orchestrator of elite habits. In envisioning and composing your story worth telling, you bring a unique ability to surpass what most of your fellow leaders bring to the table. You're not just technically good in your specialty area of sales, marketing, operations, or finance. You are a rare leader who's an expert in developing other leaders, able to raise your entire team's upside potential for high achievement. Express your full leadership power by authoring a story worth telling that stokes your passion, and contributes to developing your all-star team of collaborators.

Congratulations on drawing a line in the sand, reflected by the extraordinary choice you've made for going about your professional development: Competent is not an option.

ACKNOWLEDGEMENTS

Haley Ashland, my wife, is a deliberate practitioner of dressage, and of developing her young horse. She is always fully engaged in our ongoing conversations about deliberate practice. I admire her for taking on the years of practice needed to learn to walk, trot and - her nemesis - canter! Starting as an adult who had never ridden before was a difficult challenge, but even with the added obstacle of overcoming a loss of confidence from a terrifying fall she continues to practice daily in the pursuit of her riding dreams.

Werner Erhard, Founder of EST (which evolved into the Landmark Forum), is my model for a leader who is a mindset master. At least once a week, Haley and I acknowledge, with gratitude, the profound contribution his distinctions have made to the quality of our lives.

Big praise goes to Ken Blanchard, Chief Spiritual Officer of The Ken Blanchard Companies, for the mentoring and friendship we've shared since we met, just after *The One Minute Manager* became a best seller. I am grateful to Ken for empowering my coaching and sharing his wisdom about book publishing with me.

Pete Carroll, Head Coach of the Super-Bowl Champion Seattle Seahawks is my model for being an orchestrator of excellent habits. My experience in three years at the USC Trojan Flashback Football Camps changed forever my understanding of what it takes to develop elite talent in a business setting.

Dr. K.Anders Ericsson, Conradi Eminent Scholar and Professor of Psychology at Florida State University, is the preeminent leader of the ground-breaking research on deliberate practice. Dr. Ericsson has given me a profound gift—learning how to practice—that influences my impact with clients, my athletic abilities, and even my marriage.

Margie Adler, my elite developmental editor, worked her magic in transforming my original manuscript into a framework that is more practical and reader-friendly. My dynamic elite copy editing trio, Connie Anderson , Betty Liedtke, and Diane Keyes, took the baton from where Margie left off and cleaned up the passive voice and run on sentences. Rounding out my book production team, Alan Pranke, is a stud when it comes to cover design and interior book design. All of these pros come from the Minneapolis-St. Paul area. It took a village to bring my competent writing skills to my new magnum opus standard.

I want to acknowledge the leaders who provided me with stories worth telling: John Vuch of the St. Louis Cardinals, Gene Browne of the City Bin Company, Thom Crosby of Pal's Sudden Service, Andy Tysler of Deschutes Brewery, and Miles Reiter of Driscoll's.

Charles Herrick is one of the most multi-talented earthlings I've ever known. While we met in the heat of competition at masters track meets, he's been a great sounding board on leadership issues, and guiding me through the publishing process.

I offer a special shout out to three leaders who were the first brave souls to offer up their management teams as guinea pigs to field test the ideas in this book in Mission Unreasonable Projects. Mike Crone and Jon Boehme of Blue Bunny, and Roger Junkermier of Cerium Networks are leaders who are committed to developing their team's capacity for elite coaching.

Dr. Joe Pine saw the promise of my ideas in the book's early stages and serves as a thought leader who brings game-changing ideas to the business community.

As a track athlete, I am indebted to my team of elite coaches including Michael Waller, Duncan Atwood, Fred Luke, Tom Sinclair, Les Black, Cletus Coffey, Lance Neubauer, Jonah Silva, Mike Cunlifee, Tom Sinclair, Greg Stotsenberg, Cody Melnrick, Cricket Marshall, and Ken Troy. I appreciate their patience in coaching me to learn new athletic movements, which are not easy for a guy who can't jump rope and was a total klutz in dirty dancing classes.

I acknowledge my many training teammates in masters track, who provide me with a community that operates with a non-stop healthy disregard for the unreasonable.

Finally, I am indebted to small brigade of book reviewers/editors: Dr. Henriette Anne Klauser, Mark Rozema, Steve Miller, Bill Marvin, Christopher Brown, John Hall, Ken Lubin, Lew Schiffman, Randy Rose, Doug McAlister, Greg Bailey, Steve Hovanic, Howard Kirschenbaum, Shane Towne, Jan Dragotta, Tom Ewing, Todd

Jones, Larry Nakata, Duane Griffiths, Gail Kuhnly, Mike Salzberg, Keith Cupp, Rod Sherman, PJ Connor, Nazanin Tadjbakhsh, and Farah Allen. It's taken me so long to write this book that some of you won't recognize the content or even remember you provided feedback.

CITATIONS

Chapter 1

1. "competent." *Merriam-Webster.com*. 2011, http://www.merriam-webster.com (May 8, 2011).

2. Seth Godin, "In my Humble Opinion: In the Face of Change, the Competent are Helpless," *Fast Company*, January/February 2000, http://www.fastcompany.com/38442/change-agent-issue-31.

3. Kim Gross interview with Chris Carlisle in "Football Strength Training Secrets from USC," *Bigger, Faster, Stronger,* March/April 2006, *42-45.*

Chapter 2

1. Course Notes "Being a Leader and the Effective Exercise of Leadership: An Ontological/Phenomenological Model." Whistler, British Columbia, October, 2012.

2. Del Jones interview with Andrea Jung, "Avon's Andrea Jung: CEOs need to reinvent themselves," *USA Today*, June 15, 2009, http://usatoday30.usatoday.com/money/companies/management/advice/2009-06-14-jung-ceo-avon_N.htm?csp=N009.

3. Dr. Jim Collins, Good to Great, *Fast Company*, 2001, http://www.jimcollins.com/article_topics/articles/good-to-great.html).

4. Wendy Axelrod & Jeannie Coyle, *Make Talent Your Business.* San Francisco, Berrett-Koehler Publishers, Inc., 2011.

5. Robert Eichinger, Cara Capretta Raymond, and Jim Peters. Presentation at the 2005 Succession Management Conference. New York, (17 October 2005).

6. Hewett Associates and Human Capital Institute. *The State of Talent Management: Today's Challenges, Tomorrow's Opportunities.* Washington, DC: Human Capital Institute, 2008.

7. The original research was done at the Center for Creative Leadership by Morgan McCall, Jr, Robert W. Eichinger, and Michael M. Lombardo, and is specifically mentioned in *The Career Architect Development Planner, 3rd edition,* by Michael M. Lombardo and Robert W. Eichinger.

8. The example from Carol Burch and Chris Longridge of Girandole Enterprises comes from a phone interview in 2013 and prior conversations about their Dwaffler software.

9. Tim Gallwey, *The Inner Game of Work.* (New York: Random House), *88.*

10. Derrick Gould, "Now in Book Form: The Cardinal Way," *St. Louis Post Dispatch*, May 18, 2012, http://www.stltoday.com/sports/baseball/professional/now-in-book-form-the-cardinal-way/article_1c76331b-077e-57aa-9333-86a85b1f5ac2.html.

11. Ben Reiter, "Birds on a Power Line, *Sports Illustrated*, May 27, 2013, *69.*

12. All the information about Pal's Sudden Service came from phone interviews with CEO Thom Crosby in 2013 and 2014.

Chapter 3

1. Interview with Michael Lewis, "The Best Offense is a Stubborn Contrarian," *Fortune*, October 30, 2006, *140.*

2. Alexander Wolff. "The New Training Table." *Sports Illustrated*, November 7, 2011, *122-126.*

3. Susan Casey. "Gold Mind." *Sports Illustrated*, August 18, 2008, 44.

4. Frans Johansson, *The Medici Effect.* (Boston: Harvard Business School Press, 2004), *2.*

5. Michael Lewis, *Moneyball: The Art of Winning an Unfair Game* (New York: W.W. Norton & Company, Inc., 2004), *93.*

Chapter 4

1. Chris Broussard. "The King James Version," *ESPN The Magazine*, October, 15 2013, http://espn.go.com/nba/story/_/id/9824909/lebron-james-michael-jordan-fear-failure-35-point-games-more-espn-magazine.

2. Lee Jenkins, "Meet the rejuvenated, revitalized LeBron," *SI.com.*, April 24, 2012 http://sportsillustrated.cnn.com/2012/magazine/04/24/lebron.james/1.html.

3. Ibid.

4. Ira Winderman, "Spoelstra: LeBron can take it to greater heights," *South Florida Sun Sentinel*, April 15, 2013, http://articles.sun-sentinel.com/2013-04-15/sports/sfl-miami-heat-erik-spoelstra-s041513_1_lebron-james-brandon-jennings-erik-spoelstra.

5. President James Garfield's quote in "Pinochet's Chile : An Eyewitness Report." 1981, by Morna MacLeod, *p. 5*.

6. Walter Isaacson, *Steve Jobs* (New York: Simon & Schuster, 2001).

7. Jeremy Hunter & Michael Chaskalson. "Making the Mindful Leader: Cultivating the Skills for Facing Adaptive Challenges." Chapter accepted for publication in Leonard, S., Lewis, R., Freeman, A. & Passmore. J. (In Press). T*he Wiley-Blackwell Handbook of the Psychology of Leadership, Change & OD*. Chichester: Wiley-Blackwell.

Chapter 5

1. Geoff Colvin, "What It Takes to Be Great." *Fortune,* October 30, 2006, 93.

2. Ibid, p. 95.

3. K. Anders Ericsson's editorial, "Training history, deliberate practice and elite sports performance: an analysis in response to Tucker and Collins review—what makes champions?" *British Journal of Sports Medicine*. (June 2013), Vol. 47: no. 9, *533*.

Chapter 6

1. Malcolm Gladwell and Bill Simmons conversation on ESPN 12/20/2009.

2. James Gelles, "Basketball Fundamental - Footwork," The Coach's Clip Board, http://www.coachesclipboard.net/FootworkDrill.html.

3. Jonathan Abrams, "Bryant's Nimble Footwork is Mesmerizing the Magic," *New York Times*, June 6, 2009 http://www.nytimes.com/2009/06/07/sports/basketball/07nba.html?_r=0.

4. Charles Duhigg, *The Power of Habit: Why We Do What We Do in Life and Business.* (New York: Random House, 2012), *p.100-101.*

5. James Raley with Eric Hagerman, *Spark: The Revolutionary New Science of Exercise and the Brain.* New York: Little Brown and Company, 2008

6. Mark Bowden, *The Best Game Ever* (New York: Atlantic Monthly Press 2008). Excerpt in *Sports Illustrated*, April 28, 2008), 66.

7. Don Shula & Ken Blanchard, *The Little Book of Coaching,* (New York: Harper Collins, 2001), *p.39.*

8. John Casteele, "What Ballet Does for Football," AZ Central.com, http://healthyliving.azcentral.com/ballet-football-1747.html.

9. Chris Ballard, *The Art of a Beautiful Game,* (New York: Simon & Schuster, 2009), *p. 30-32.*

10. Captain "Sully" Sullenberger, *Highest Duty*, (New York: Harper Collins, 2009), *p. 313-314.*

11. Mike Krzyzewski, *Leading with the Heart.* (New York: Warner Books, 2000), *p. 27.*

Chapter 7

1. Phil Jackson, *Eleven Rings: The Soul of Success*. (New York: The Penguin Press, 2013), *p. 23-24.*

2. All of the material on Coach Nick Saban's player development process at the University of Alabama comes from four primary sources:

    Ben Cohen & Rachel Bachman, "How Saban Turned the Tide," *Wall Street Journal*, April 28, 2012.

    Stewart Mandel and Andy Staples, "Go For It on Fourth and Multiply" *Sports Illustrated*, June 10, 2013, *p. 46-50.*

    Andy Staples, "The Sabinization of College Football." *Sports Illustrated*, August 12, 2012.

    Tim Layden, "Heir Force," *Sports Illustrated,* January 14, 2013, *p. 32-37.*

    Brian O'Keefe, "Leadership Lessons from Nick Saban," *Fortune Magazine* September 7, 2012, http://money.cnn.com/2012/09/07/news/companies/alabama-coach-saban.fortune/index.html.

3. The content related to Pete Carroll's player development process at USC came from two sources. Speeches by Coach Carroll and the coaching staff and practice field experience during USC Trojan Flashball Football Camps, (June 2006, 2007, 2008). The second source was from Pete Carroll. Yogi Roth. and Kristoffer A. Garin, *Win Forever: Live, Work, and Play Like a Champion,* (New York: Portfolio/Penguin, 2011).

4. Teresa Amabile and Steve Kramer, "Small Wins and Feeling Good." *Harvard Business Review*, May 13, 2011.

5. Verne Harnish, *Mastering the Rockefeller Habits.* (New York: Select Books, Inc), 2002.

6. All the information about The City Bin Company came from e-mail exchanges with Founder and CEO, Gene Browne.

7. Quotivee, "20 quotes by Mark Cuban That Tell the Secret of Winning," January 27. 2014, http://quotivee.com/2014/articles/20-quotes-by-mark-cuban-that-tell-the-secret-of-winning/

Chapter 8

1. Dale Schunk & Barry Zimmerman (Ed). *Self-regulation of Learning and Performance: Issues and Educational Applications,* (Hillsdale, NJ, England: Lawrence Erlbaum Associates, Inc., 1994).

2. Greg Olson shared this information about a turning point in the mindset of the Atlanta Braves team during a phone interview.

3. All the information about Driscoll's came from interviews with Founder and CEO, Miles Reiter, and my own participation as a trainer in the Driscoll's Leadership Institute.

4. David A Garvin, "The US Army's After Action Reviews: Seizing the Chance to Learn." An excerpt from *"Learning In Action, A Guide to Putting the Learning Organization to Work"* (Boston: Harvard Business School Press, 2000), *106-116.*

5. All the information about Deschutes Brewery's sales organization came from phone interviews, e-mails exchanges, and seminar interactions with VP of Sales, Andy Tysler.

6. All the information about Blue Bunny's sales organization came from phone interviews, e-mails exchanges, and seminar interactions with VP of Sales, Mike Crone.

CONTACT ART

To get the latest updates on *Competent is Not an Option* including tools and Art's *Game-Changer blog*, visit: **www.turock.com**

Speeches and Seminars.

Art customizes 1 hour, half-day, full-day speech or interactive seminar versions of this content, depending on your needs. To find out more, visit:

www.turock.com/speeches-and-seminars
www.turock.com/about-art/videos

Mission Unreasonable Projects.

These projects aren't for those not truly committed to 'elite' performance, those doing fine pursing Mission 'Walk-in-the-Park' or Mission 'Tiddlywinks.' These year-long projects are designed for executive teams who are taking on new responsibilities and realize the winning formulas responsible for their past success will undermine their future success.

www.turock.com/coaching-and-projects/leadership-development-projects

Executive Coaching.

As you can tell from the coaching examples in this book, Art's executive coaching produces immediate openings for breakthroughs in performance in a single conversation. To get more details:

www.turock.com/coaching-and-projects/executive-coaching

Organizational assessments.

Art interacts with leadership teams that desire to develop elite leaders but lack the skills and knowledge to do so efficiently. Download Art's *"Conditions for Leadership Development Audit,"* to help your management team assess the gaps between your current leadership development process and the elite case examples described in this book. Available at:

www.turock.com/tools

Send this questionnaire to your key executives to fill out. Arrange a conference call with Art to turn the findings into improvements that saturate your organization with elite leaders.

Connect with Art through social media.

Google "Art Turock Linkedin" to join Art's Linkedin contacts and indicate in your invitation that you've read this book.
Read Art's periodic posts located in Linkedin groups such as *Chief Learning Officer, Sports Business Journal, Executive Athletes,* and *Executive Suite.*

ELITE PERFORMER'S GUIDE TO SHARING VALUBLE BOOKS

If you found this book to be valuable, then apply the Learning-While-Working Model by practicing *P/4 Perfect* and *P/5 Publicize*

Step 1: Ask yourself, "Who else would benefit from the lessons I've learned in this book? Create a list or contacts filter in your contact management system. Think of team members, colleagues in other departments, trade association buddies, social media groups, and especially your boss or the owner of your business. (P5)

Step 2: Prepare an e-mail that summarizes your key mindset disturbances and actionable ideas you gained from reading this book. Share with your answers to questions like: What fictitious difficulties that have limited your performance no longer seem significant? What are the skill sets and facets of your performance where you now doing deliberate practice? (P4)

Step 3: In your e-mail, include this link **www.turock.com/tools** to the following tools and services:
- Condensed version of the book
- Organizational assessment, "Conditions for Leadership Development Audit"
- Coaching call with Art
  www.turock.com/coaching-and-projects/executive-coaching/

Step 4: Copy Art on the e-mail you send to your contacts. He wants to learn about the results readers, like you, take away from reading *Competent is Not an Option.* (P5)

Step 5: Order ten or more copies at a generous discount by calling 425-814-3038.

CHAPTER 88

ABOUT ART TUROCK

Art Turock is an elite performance game-changer who helps clients develop elite leaders, achieve unprecedented productivity, and ignite their hidden leadership capacity. His delivers keynote speeches, seminars, executive coaching, and year-long Mission Unreasonable Projects.

Art has been a valued resource to over 120 *Fortune* 500 companies, including 3M, Procter & Gamble, Harley-Davidson, and Fed-Ex. He has spoken to hundreds of trade associations and executive education groups such as the American Society of Association Executives and Young Presidents' Organization. Articles by Art, and references to his work, have appeared in *Success, USA Today, Fortune, Reader's Digest, Association Management, Chicken Soup for the Soul at Work*, Bloomberg News, CNN, the HBO/Sports Illustrated documentary, "Sport in America," and even on a Starbuck's cup in "The Way I See It" series.

Art's viewpoint about talent development in business is heavily influenced by his background in sports. Art took up competitive sprinting at age 56 and pentathlon at age 61. He achieved an All-American standard time in the 60-meter indoor dash. In 2011, his pentathlon score ranked #4 in the United States for his competitive age group. Over a period of three years, Art spent eleven days immersed in fantasy camps and attending team practices to study the Win Forever coaching philosophy of Coach Pete Carroll and the USC Trojans.

Art has written two books, *Invent Business Opportunities No One Else Can Imagine* and *Getting Physical: How to Stick With Your Exercise Program.*

His first leadership experience involved being Training Project Coordinator for the Interpersonal Skills Training Project based at the University of Iowa College of Medicine.

Art Turock graduated from Union College (BS) and the University of Florida (M.Ed.). He is a member of Phi Beta Kappa Honor Society and USA Track & Field Association.